NORTHWEST VOICES

Northwest Voices

LANGUAGE AND CULTURE
IN THE PACIFIC NORTHWEST

Edited by Kristin Denham

Oregon State University Press   Corvallis

Library of Congress Cataloging-in-Publication Data

Names: Denham, Kristin E., 1967- editor.
Title: Northwest voices : language and culture in the Pacific Northwest /
   edited by Kristin Denham.
Description: Corvallis : Oregon State University Press, 2019. | Includes
   bibliographical references and index.
Identifiers: LCCN 2018055310 | ISBN 9780870719639 (original trade pbk. :
   alk. paper)
Subjects: LCSH: Indians of North America—Northwest Coast of North
   America—Languages. | Northwest Coast of North America—Languages.
   | Northwest, Pacific—Languages. | Language and culture—Northwest,
   Pacific.
Classification: LCC PM481 .N67 2019 | DDC 306.4409795—dc23
LC record available at https://lccn.loc.gov/2018055310

♾ This paper meets the requirements of ANSI/NISO Z39.48-1992
(Permanence of Paper).

Oregon State University Press
121 The Valley Library
Corvallis OR 97331-4501
541-737-3166 • fax 541-737-3170
www.osupress.oregonstate.edu

Contents

PART 1
Historical Background of the Region
KRISTIN DENHAM

In chapters 1 and 2, the authors provide the historical background necessary to understand the linguistic situation of a region and its peoples. In chapter 1, "Linguistic Diversity in Oregon and Washington," Edwin Battistella and David Pippin offer us a history of the Pacific Northwest region—the areas we now call Oregon and Washington, though they have only relatively recently acquired those state names. In chapter 2, "Place-Names of the Pacific Northwest," Allan Richardson provides an overview of the region, its history, its settlement patterns, and the widespread influences from the many diverse Indigenous groups and their languages through a thorough exploration of place-names.

Even calling the region the "Pacific Northwest" assumes country boundaries that have been established only relatively recently. In 1846, the United States and Britain signed the Treaty of Oregon, which established the 49th parallel as the international boundary in the Pacific Northwest. The region, including what is now Oregon, Washington, Idaho, and large areas of British Columbia, had been jointly occupied by Britain and the United States. But after 1846, the 49th parallel established an international boundary. Oregon then became one of the United States in 1859, and Washington not until thirty years later, in 1889. The groups of Indigenous peoples living in the region had, of course, not recognized an international boundary and had long made their homes, their fishing grounds, and their settlements throughout the region, including on the many islands in what we now call the Salish Sea.

An understanding of the various groups who have lived in this region for millennia and of those who occupied, passed through, settled, and now call it home gives us insight into the languages they speak and have spoken, and the ways in which those languages serve as important reminders not only of the distant past, but also of the more recent past. An understanding of the past, as we know, is critical to understanding our present and our future.

1

Linguistic Diversity in Oregon and Washington

EDWIN BATTISTELLA AND DAVID PIPPIN

One of the goals of language research is to explore linguistic diversity and language variation. Often though, these terms may seem to be abstractions, particularly when our understanding of diversity is grounded against a background of ingrained prescriptivism and standard language mythology.

To foster a more fine-grained understanding, we can bring local historical and demographic research into play. By investigating the history of language in a region—in this case, Oregon and Washington—we can engage with the linguistic history of our own communities (and in many cases our own backgrounds) and come to think about language diversity in the context of regional historical forces. Exploring language history requires some background and perspective, of course, and providing that is the goal of this chapter. We begin at the beginning, with the languages of Native peoples.

THE EARLIEST LANGUAGES

The earliest languages spoken in the Northwest were those of immigrants from northeast Asia, traveling across the continental shelf into what is now Alaska and Canada, making their way along the Pacific Coast and inland, and then moving to the Great Plains. As a result, the Northwest generally shows dense language concentrations of pre-European languages, and the archeological record dates back as far as 13,500 years. The presence of archeological sites in the interior regions of the Northwest, compared with the paucity of sites along the coast, suggested for early scholars a westward migration from the Columbia Plateau to the coast. Anthropologists underestimated the length of human occupation in the Northwest, and so the westward movement theories were used to explain the rich linguistic diversity of the region. With the acceptance of a longer human presence in the Northwest, it becomes possible to account for linguistic variation within the region without that diversity being dependent on movement into the area (see Suttles 1987).

Many First Nations groups remained in the Pacific Northwest, and the region is home to not only many languages but also many language *families*. Moving north to south, Native language families of the Pacific Northwest include Athabaskan, Tlingit, Tsimshian, Haida, Wakashan, Salishan, Chimacuan, Plateau Penutian, Lower Columbia River Penutian (Chinookan), Coosan, and Uto-Aztecan. At the beginning of the nineteenth century, fourteen language families were represented in Oregon alone, more than any comparably sized geographical region (Loy et al. 2001; see also Gross 2007 and Berg 2007).

The once-robust Native languages lost speakers from disease, colonialism, and assimilationist language policies. Smallpox, "fever and ague" (malaria), and measles laid waste to village populations in the late eighteenth and nineteenth centuries (see Boyd 1999). The treaty process forced diverse tribes onto joint reservations, and in both Washington and Oregon, Native resistance incurred an armed response from the US government. The Rogue River Indian Wars of 1855–1856, for example, resulted in many Native Americans being dispossessed to the Siletz and Grand Ronde Reservations west of Salem, often far from their traditional lands. By the late nineteenth century, most tribes were restricted to reservations, and many children were taken to English-only boarding schools such as the Tulalip Indian Boarding School in Washington and the United States Indian Industrial and Training School in Forest Grove, Oregon (see Collins 1998 and Adams 1995 for more on the boarding-school experience). Already threatened by loss of population, Native languages were increasingly being eradicated through federal policy.

More recently, the 1950s saw the United States ending its federal trusteeship with many of the tribes, a process known as "termination." In Washington State, several tribes, including the Duwamish of Seattle, remain unrecognized, but no tribes were terminated, quite surprising since Senator Henry Jackson (D-WA) was a sponsor of the original resolution to end federal trusteeship. In Oregon, by contrast, sixty-two Native groups lost their status. A few tribes remained federally recognized during this period, such as the Confederated Tribes of Warm Springs, the Confederated Tribes of Umatilla, and the Burns Paiute Tribe. Others have since reestablished federal recognition and sovereignty: the Confederated Tribes of Siletz in 1977; the

Cow Creek Band of the Umpqua Tribe in 1982; the Confederated Tribes of the Grand Ronde Community of Oregon in 1983; the Coos, Lower Umpqua, and Siuslaw in 1984; the Klamath Tribes in 1986; and the Coquille Indian Tribes in 1989 (see Fixico 2018 for more details, and Fixico 1986 for a broader study of federal policy).

Today nine tribes are federally recognized in Oregon (of a total of 566 tribes nationally), the majority in western Oregon. In 2014, the nine tribes had a total enrolled membership of 27,433, though in the 2010 census, 109,223 people identified themselves as American Indian and Alaska Native. Washington State has twenty-nine federally recognized tribes, and seven not yet recognized. As for speakers of the languages, according to the American Community Language Survey data (released in 2015), 2,151 people in Oregon reported speaking a Native American language, with more than one hundred people indicating Klamath, Nez Perce, Sahaptian, Upper Chinook, Dakota, Cherokee, and Mono (US Census Bureau 2015). Out of the 4,167 speakers of Native languages in Washington State, 815 reported speaking a Sahaptian language, the language group of the Columbia Plateau tribes. The Salishan languages—Spokane, Kalispel, and Flathead—are represented by 670 speakers. Languages of the Coast Salish people of Western Washington—primarily Lushootseed—are lumped together in the survey as Puget Sound Salish, and 135 people reported speaking one of these languages at home. Moving farther west, more than one hundred people in each tribe reported speaking a language of the Northwest Coast, including Makah, Kwakwaka'wakw (Kwakiutl), Klallam, and Quinault. The American Community Language Survey also suggests that Navajo and Cherokee are also spoken in Washington by several hundred speakers each.

Notable too is Chinook Jargon, a pidgin language that is also sometimes referred to as Chinook Pidgin, Chinuk Wawa, or Tsinuk Wawa. It was used as a lingua franca in contact times, but its origins as a pre- or post-contact pidgin are still a matter of scholarly debate. See Lang (2008) for more on the genesis of Chinook Jargon. Reservation life, in which speakers of different tribes lived together in a common area, led to the development of the creole form, known as Chinuk Wawa, spoken extensively by the Grande Ronde community (see Zenk and Cole, this volume).

Today, the economic stability brought about by restoration of sovereignty has established a resource base for language preservation, reclamation, and restoration. Efforts include teacher training, pedagogy, documentation of language and culture, immersion projects, and university language classes in Lushootseed, Chinuk Wawa, and Ichishkíin. High schools, too, offer instruction in Native languages. In Washington State, for example, a survey conducted in 2009 by the University of Washington showed that seven high schools offer a Native language class, as many as offer classes in Japanese, Arabic, Russian, or Latin. (For more on language efforts by tribes, see the work of Lushootseed Research; projects listed at the Northwest Indian Language Institute at the University of Oregon; and the papers in Gross 2007).

EUROPEAN-NATIVE CONTACT

Europeans were motivated to learn Native languages until the population of white settlers outnumbered that of Native people. It was the railroad that changed the balance, but first contact by Europeans came by sea. By the mid-1500s, Spanish galleons had landed along the coast of Northern California, and as early as 1543, Bartolomé Ferrelo may have sailed as far north as the Oregon-California border. By 1603, Sebastián Vizcaíno, a Basque sailing for Spain, reached the coast of Oregon at what is now named Cape Sebastian, near present-day Gold Beach, Oregon. Today, many places still bear Spanish names, most notably islands in the San Juan and Gulf Islands archipelagos, but after the eighteenth century Spanish influence in this area diminished (for more on the place-names of the Pacific Northwest, see Allan Richardson, this volume). Russian explorers and fur traders were also a presence, and they were a concern for the viceroyalty of New Spain. Worried that Russia might challenge their predominance in the Pacific Northwest, in the late 1700s the Spanish began establishing a series of missions, forts, and villages extending north to San Francisco. However, it was the Americans and British who would contest the region during the first part of the nineteenth century.

James Cook was the first English captain to discover the extraordinary price that Chinese merchants were willing to pay for sea otter pelts. In 1778, on his third voyage to the Pacific, he sailed his ships, HMS *Resolution* and HMS *Discovery*, to the central Oregon coast, named Cape Flattery in Washington State (the oldest non-Native name in the state) and, in March of that year, made contact with Native people in the village of Yuquot on the west coast of present-day Vancouver Island. It was his misunderstanding of the word *nuutkah* ('to turn around') that resulted in the name "Nootka" for the inlet that they entered and the people they encountered. In 1979 the West Coast Allied Tribes changed the name of the collected people of this region to Nuu-chah-nulth, but in Cook's day it is likely that the people referred to themselves and their language as "Takaht," meaning, "straight or correct (i.e., correctly speaking) people, in contradistinction to 'Owsuppaht,' by which they designate all those whose speech they do not understand. 'Tahkaht' is a term of honour, and 'Owsuppaht' of reproach, like Greek and Barbarian in ancient times" (Knipe 1868). The maritime fur trade that developed there flourished for another forty years until the decline of the otter population in the 1820s. By then the fur trade had moved inland and southward in pursuit of beaver pelts along the Columbia River.

Cook developed a short vocabulary of Native words and mistakenly assumed that they would be understood by people in the entire region. He was wrong about the uniformity of language in the region, but his presence nevertheless led to the creation of a trade language—Nootka Jargon—that later contributed to the pidgin used in the Lower Columbia. Examples of words from the west coast of Vancouver Island that wound up in Chinook Jargon are *wik* 'no, not,' and *wawa* 'to speak, talk.' The Nootka Sound was also the scene of a diplomatic crisis that had a lasting impact on the region: as the fur trade expanded, Spain captured several English ships, and the English prepared for war. The crisis was resolved peacefully through a series of agreements—from 1790 to 1795—and Spain ceded control of the Pacific Northwest, both politically and linguistically.

MULTILINGUALISM IN THE LOWER COLUMBIA

In 1792, Captain Robert Gray of Rhode Island sailed into the mouth of the Columbia River, not past it as George Vancouver had done earlier that same year. Gray renamed it after his ship, the *Columbia Rediviva*. The famous expedition of Lewis and Clark and the founding of Astoria in 1811 helped further establish the American presence in the Pacific Northwest. One of the earliest recorded sentences of Chinuk Wawa occurred in December 1805 when Captain William Clark was hunting ducks with his musket. After shooting a duck, Clark reported that a Clatsop person said,

Clouch musket, wake come ma-tax musket.
'That is a good musket, I do not understand this musket.'

Apart from the word *musket*, all these words would be intelligible to speakers of Nootka Jargon. Clark was kinder than most in describing the sound system of what he thought was the Clatsop language. He suggested that it was "resembling ours in pronunciation & more easy to learn than [Lower Chinook]" (Lang 2008, 15). Meriwether Lewis put together a Chinookan vocabulary that he later lost in a boating accident on the Potomac, but two men traveling with him also developed lists, and one of them, Alexander Ross, included a list of "another lingo, or rather mixed dialect, spoken by the Chinook and neighboring tribes; which is generally used in their intercourse with the whites" (Lang 2008, 56).

From 1818 to 1846, the Oregon Territory was jointly occupied by British and Americans, and an important center for that occupation was Fort Vancouver, located along the Columbia River in present-day Vancouver, Washington. Among the many different languages one might have heard at Vancouver were French, Mohawk, Scots, Métis, Cree, English, Nez Perce, Paiute, Bannock, Shoshone, Yakama, Klickitat, Cowlitz, Chinookan, and Hawaiian. It is estimated that, in 1844, a hundred Hawaiians lived in "Kanaka Town" of Fort Vancouver—*kanaka* is the Hawaiian word for "person" and became the widely used Chinook Jargon word for Hawaiians—but another three hundred Hawaiians worked for Hudson's Bay Company along the rest of the Columbia. Because most Hawaiians there were men, many married into Native families. By the time of statehood for Oregon, the population of Hawaiians had declined precipitously. Carlton Clark suggests that many Hawaiian laborers held temporary contracts and never intended to stay in the Oregon Territory but doesn't mention the effect of racist laws that imposed taxes on "Chinese, Hawaiians, and Mulattos" and a ban on interracial marriage. Both may have contributed to the decline in the population of Hawaiians. Today the Hawaiian community makes its presence known over the airwaves and in cultural events throughout the Pacific Northwest. Hawaiian words can also be found in place-names throughout the region: the town of Kalama, Washington (named for John Kalama), Kanaka Bay on the south side of San Juan Island, and numerous places on Salt Spring Island in British Columbia.

THE US EXPLORING EXPEDITION AND AMERICAN SETTLEMENT OF THE OREGON TERRITORY

The US Exploring Expedition (1838–1842) was an American survey of the Pacific Ocean and, importantly, the first systematic study of Pacific Northwest languages. Horatio Hale, the ethnographer-philologist, was the leader of this effort. His language map of the region is a thing of beauty, and the volume that he published after the voyage contains numerous word list and notes on the grammars of Native languages. By Hale's time, Europeans and Americans had been in the region for more than sixty years and had resolved the question of whether or not there was a Northwest Passage from Europe to Asia. In just five more years, the territory would be divided between both groups to the exclusion of the original inhabitants. The Oregon Treaty of 1846 fixed the boundary between Great Britain and the United States at the 49th parallel.

Once the border was established, American settlement in the Oregon Territory took off and, with the creation of the Washington Territory in 1851, the process of treaty-making began. The early settlements in French Prairie, Tualatin Plains, and the Chehalem Valley had already extended to the Willamette Valley by 1843, and emigrants soon made their way to Umpqua Valley by 1849. Who were these early settlers? In *The Willamette Valley: Migration and Settlement on the Oregon Frontier*, William Bowen writes that those settling on the so-called urban frontier tended to be "disproportionately from the ranks of unmarried men from the Northeast or abroad" (1978, 53). The census of 1850 recorded 11,873 Oregonians, 60 percent of whom were males and most of whom hailed from the states of Maine, Massachusetts, New York, Pennsylvania, Virginia, North Carolina, Kentucky, Tennessee, and Ohio (Loy et al. 2001, 15; see also Richardson, this volume). According to Randall Mills, writing in *American Speech*, most settlers funneled through the Missouri and Iowa areas while preparing to travel west on the Oregon Trail. The migration brought a cohesive language to the new territory, incorporating the speech of many emigrants from New England or New York (Mills 1950, 83). Mills goes on to suggest three broad dialect areas: a narrow strip along the Willamette River from Portland to Eugene, a more rural area extending from the Willamette River Valley to the Pacific Coast Range, and an area to the east of the Cascade Mountains and to the south of the Calapooya Mountains.

Early newspaper reports give clues not just to who settled here, but to the ways in which settlers viewed language. The *Oregon Spectator*, the first American newspaper to be published on the Pacific Coast, ran from 1846 to 1855, and its records contain a wealth of regional and dialect terms (including borrowings from Chinook Jargon) as well as editorial commentary about the language of competing newspapers such as the *Oregon Statesman* (founded in 1851) and the *Oregonian* (founded in 1850). Among the terms from the *Spectator* cited by Mills are representations of dialect pronunciations like "cheer," "drother," "fortin," "garden sars," "idee," "kittle," "Ioway," and "Californey" (for *chair, I'd rather, fourteen, garden sauce (garden salad), idea, kettle, Iowa, and California*) and terms such as *absquatulate, cross-timber, dog-cheap, fixins, nary, right jam to,* and *right smart,* as well as words like *cumtux, ictas, muckamuck,* and *tillicum* from Chinook Jargon.[1]

The Donation Land Claim Act of 1850 was a crucial factor in southern and eastern expansion—the areas beyond the Willamette Valley. The act legitimized earlier 640-acre claims in the Willamette Valley and offered land claims of 320 acres to white male citizens and their wives, dispossessing Native Americans and excluding nonwhites. Later fueled by the discovery of gold in Southern Oregon, the act caused an influx of white settlers to the Umpqua and Rogue Valleys, eventually culminating in the Rogue River Indian Wars. As William Robbins explains, "The consequence was something akin to a race war in 1852 and 1853, with white volunteer forces ruthlessly driving Indians from their traditional hunting and gathering grounds" (Robbins 2018). Hostilities culminated in the Battle of Hungry Hill in 1855, after which most of the Rogue River Indians were removed to the Siletz and Grande Ronde Reservations. Native people north of the Columbia were subject to the same treatment as those in Oregon, with multiple tribes forced into confederated groups on the Colville and Tulalip Reservations. Free land and Indian removal caused Oregon's European American population to grow, increasing from 11,873 in 1850 to some 60,000 by 1860 (Robbins 2018). By 1900, just forty-one years into statehood, the census reported 418,636 people in Oregon, nearly a quarter of whom lived in Multnomah County, where Portland is located.

AFRICAN AMERICANS IN OREGON AND WASHINGTON

The Oregon provisional government and the 1857 Oregon Constitution banned slavery but also excluded African Americans from residing legally, owning property, making contracts, voting, or using the legal system. Oregon's was the only state constitution to do so, and the provision remained in effect until 1926. As a result of the historically inhospitable atmosphere, as well as the restriction of the Donation Land Claims Act to white settlers, the number of African Americans in the Oregon Territory remained small.

One of the African Americans denied entry into the territory was George Washington Bush. Originally from Missouri, he had fled that state because of a restriction barring free blacks from living there. In 1844 he crossed the Columbia and settled in what would soon become the Washington Territory (1853). The whites-only clause of the Donation Land Claims Act made conflict likely, but Bush's neighbors supported him. In March of the following year, the Territorial Legislature asked for an exception to the Donation Land Claims Act so that George Washington Bush could purchase the land he had settled along Puget Sound:

> The Legislative Assembly of the Territory of Washington . . . would most respectfully represent unto your honorable body, that George Bush, a free mulatto, with his wife and children, emigrated to, and settled in, now Washington Territory, Thurston County, in the year 1845 (Millner 1998,16).

In the early twentieth century, the railroad and the emergence of Portland as a travel and business center created employment opportunities for African Americans; the Pearl District of Portland developed as an ethnic neighborhood; and the city became the home of the first NAACP chapter west of the Mississippi in 1914. Darrell Millner notes that, in the early twentieth century, coal mining, ranching, logging, and railroad work brought African Americans to towns such as Coos Bay, Pendleton, Maxville, and LaGrande. Later, military activity fostered African American communities in Pendleton and Klamath Falls, as well as Portland, where the African American population grew from two thousand in 1940 to twenty-two thousand in 1944 (Millner 2018). Nevertheless, the percentage of African Americans was still less than 1 percent until the 1960s. And in the 2010 census, the figure was at about only 2 percent, an estimated sixty-nine thousand people. There is little research specifically on African American speech in Oregon, though such topics as the history of Portland's Albina community and the local histories of railroad, ranching, logging, and military towns might prove to be fruitful in identifying representations of speech and in documenting language attitudes (see McLagan 1980 and Taylor 1998 for more on the migration of African Americans to Oregon).

EUROPEAN IMMIGRATION

Many of the early white settlers of Oregon spoke German or French,[2] and later, during the period from 1890 to 1910, German and Canadian immigration was particularly high. Loy et al. (2001, 40) report that in 1890 German immigrants accounted for more than 5 percent of the population in three Oregon counties and 2–4.9 percent in twelve others. German is still widely spoken in the state, and German, Austrian, and Swiss immigrants have influenced areas such as Mount Angel, Metzger, Salem, and Portland. At the same time, Astoria developed a large Finnish population. Other Scandinavian immigrants arrived there overland from the Midwest or directly from Norway and Sweden. Railroads, lumber, and fishing provided many of the jobs for these immigrants. Although the original immigrants could get by without learning English, subsequent generations would rely less on the ancestral language.

Surprisingly, or perhaps not, Russian is the third or fourth most spoken language in Oregon, behind English and Spanish and essentially tied with Vietnamese. In Washington State it ranks similarly—fourth—just ahead of Tagalog, a language of the Philippines. Russians have settled in the Pacific Northwest since the late 1700s and were in the area before even Lewis and Clark. Tatiana Osipovich of Lewis and Clark College has documented a wave of Russian immigrants arriving after the sale of Alaska to the United States in 1867, leading to Oregon's first Russian Orthodox Church, St. Nicholas Russian Orthodox Church in Portland. Later groups of Russians arrived in Oregon and Washington in the 1880s and 1920s and in the last quarter of the twentieth century, primarily Russian Jews fleeing persecution under Stalin, Orthodox Russians fleeing communism, and a variety of Russian-speaking groups resettling after the fall of the Soviet Union. In 1971, about three thousand Russian Orthodox Old Believers emigrated from Brazil to Portland.[3] Today, about one hundred thousand Russian speakers live in Oregon, most in the Portland metro area. The number of Russian refugees entering the United States has declined in recent years, but conflict in Ukraine has led to an increased number of refugees from that region. According to the Office of Refugee Resettlement in Washington, DC, Washington State leads the nation in refugees from Ukraine—467 in 2015.

LINGUISTIC INFLUENCES FROM ASIA: CHINESE, JAPANESE, FILIPINO, AND VIETNAMESE IMMIGRATION

As with the European immigrants, Asian immigration to the Pacific Northwest was associated with extraction of the area's abundant natural resources. Chinese immigration was especially significant, and Cantonese speakers from southeast China were the earliest Chinese immigrants. Primarily miners, they settled in Josephine and Jackson Counties in southwest Oregon, northeastern Oregon, Seattle, and Tacoma. As Douglas Lee shows in his "Chinese Americans in Oregon" (2018), from the mid-1860s, the Cantonese population began finding opportunities outside the mines, settling around the state. The number of Chinese in Oregon rose steadily, to more than ten thousand in 1900, with Portland then home to the second-largest Chinatown in the United States (Lee 2018). The coming of the railroad brought even more Chinese laborers to the Pacific Northwest. As the Chinese population grew, so did racist sentiment. Worried about immigrants taking away jobs during the economic distress of the 1860s and 1870s, Congress enacted the Page Act of 1878 and the Chinese Exclusion Act of 1882.[4] Anti-Chinese mobs in Tacoma drove Chinese laborers from their homes onto trains bound for Portland's Chinatown, which had also been the refuge of Chinese living elsewhere in Oregon. This discrimination, coupled with the fact that many Chinese immigrants were male sojourners, not intending to stay in America, led to the creation of an insular community that resisted acculturation.

Not until the Immigration and Naturalization Act of 1965 would significantly more Chinese immigrate to the Pacific Northwest (often by way of California), representing a greater linguistic diversity than did the original Cantonese settlements. In addition, as the twenty-first century approached, increasing numbers of Chinese Americans also moved to the Pacific Northwest, establishing Chinese Americans as one of the largest ethnic groups in the region.

After the Chinese Exclusion Act went into effect, labor contractors turned to Japan for workers, with more than three thousand Japanese workers, mostly single men, immigrating. Over time, these Issei (as this first-generation group was called) brought spouses and built families. Concentrations of Japanese families developed in Milwaukie, Hood River, Gresham, Banks, Salem, and an area known as Japantown in Portland from 1890 to 1942. In the early twentieth century, one-quarter to two-thirds of Oregon's Japanese population was involved in farm labor and agriculture. After 1923, however, such laws as the Oregon Alien Land Law and the federal Immigration Act of 1924 institutionalized anti-Japanese discrimination. Nearly two decades later, discrimination would give way to hysteria when Franklin Delano Roosevelt's Executive Order 9066 led to the internment of Japanese Americans from Oregon in relocation centers in

Minidoka, Idaho; Tule Lake, California; and Heart Mountain, Wyoming. In 1945, the Supreme Court closed the camps and most Japanese Americans in Oregon returned to the towns where they had lived, but often faced open discrimination and hostility, fueled by organizations like the Gresham-based Japanese Exclusion League.

The Pacific Northwest is also home to a large Filipino population. After the Philippine-American War ended in 1902, the Philippines became an American colony, and as US nationals, Filipinos were able to immigrate when other Asians were excluded by discriminatory immigration laws. Seattle received the largest number of Filipinos, and, as in the Chinese groups before them, men far outnumbered women. Men started mingling with white women at taxi-dance halls, and not long after that legislators introduced anti-miscegenation laws. The Filipino community fought back, and neither of the two attempts to ban intermarriage during the 1930s was successful. According to Strandjord, it was "by appropriating American themes of egalitarianism and anchoring their arguments in the language of the Declaration of Independence and the United States Constitution, [that] Filipino writers asserted their own American identity in their arguments for intermarriage" (2009). Today in the Puget Sound region there are roughly sixty thousand speakers of Tagalog and other languages of the Philippines such as Bisayan, Sebuano, Pangasinan, Ilocano, Bikol, and Pampangan. It wasn't too long ago that Filipinos, or Igorrotes, were displayed as curiosities in the Alaska-Yukon-Pacific Exposition. There may not be a Manilatown in Seattle, but by connecting for conversation in such places as Seafood City south of Seattle, the Filipino community keeps a multilingual heritage alive.

More recently, the Southeast Asian and Asian American population in the Pacific Northwest has grown following the Vietnam War. In the 1970s, Washington governor Dan Evans welcomed Vietnamese refugees when other leaders, like California's Jerry Brown, would not. Oregon, too, welcomed the South Vietnamese, who would have faced persecution had they stayed in Vietnam. Today many Vietnamese live in the suburbs of Portland, the areas known as the West Hills and Happy Valley and the towns of Aloha and Beaverton. Many Vietnamese and Vietnamese Americans have also moved to other smaller cities such as Salem, Springfield, and Medford. Currently, Vietnamese is the most widely spoken Asian language in both Oregon and Washington and second to Spanish in overall number of speakers.

SPANISH COMES BACK TO THE PACIFIC NORTHWEST

The first Mexican in the Pacific Northwest came to the region when Mexico was still part of New Spain. José Mariano Moziño produced a biological survey for the Malaspina Expedition of 1789–1794, called *Noticias de Nootka*. The Spanish may have abandoned the Pacific Northwest after the Nootka Convention, but Mexican independence in 1821 and the US conquest of Mexico's northern territory in 1848 ushered in new Spanish-language influences to Oregon and Washington. Spanish and Mexican horsemen, packers, and herders (known as *vaqueros*) made their way to eastern Oregon and the Illinois Valley and to towns like Oregon City. Mining, not the fur trade, was where Mexican mule packers made their contributions, and in 1870 Walla Walla, Washington, had a sizable Mexican population. Mexicans were exempted from the 1917 Immigration Act and according to Garcia (2018), the number of permanent residents of Mexican ancestry in Oregon grew from 569 in the 1920 census to 1,568 by 1930, though the census figures did not reflect the migrant labor force. In the 1930s, as the Great Depression fueled economic resentment and the US government instituted its so-called Repatriation Program, many Mexicans in the Pacific Northwest settled in rural areas. During World War II, more than fifteen thousand laborers from Mexico came to the region under the Bracero Program, which lasted from 1942 to 1947. Owing to the displacement of Japanese Americans to concentration camps during World War II, the Bracero Program was especially important to farmers in Washington State. After World War II, Chicano immigrants from Texas and California replaced immigrants from Mexico. By the 1950s, Mexican Americans had established communities in Nyssa, Hood River, Woodburn, and Independence, growing to a population of about thirty-two thousand by 1970 and sixty-five thousand in 1980 (Garcia 2018).

The Yakima Valley is the center of Washington's Mexican American population. Mexican Americans make up the majority of the population there and recently scored a victory to redistrict the city council districts to allow for majority Latinx districts. Chicano workers in that area have long worked to make their political voices heard. They launched "wildcat strikes" in 1969–1970, set up health clinics, and in 1979 established the Spanish-language public radio station KDNA, La Voz del Campesino. Latinx people have moved to urban areas west of the mountains, as well, with Seattle and Mount Vernon being important destinations. In 2004 the Latinx population of King County was 117,000, close to 6 percent Latinx.

According to the 2010 census, Oregon's Hispanic population (the term used in the census) was 450,052, with about 85 percent of Mexican origin. Garcia reports that the highest concentration of Latinxs in Oregon in the twenty-first century has been in towns with historic immigrant populations, and five cities have majority Latinx populations: Gervais, Boardman, Nyssa, Woodburn, and Cornelius (see also Gamboa and Baun 1995; and Bussell 2008). In addition, cities such as Hillsboro, Gresham, Beaverton, Bend, Hermiston, Umatilla, and Salem also have seen increases in Latinx populations (Garcia 2018).

Among the Spanishes to be found in the Pacific Northwest are varieties from the Dominican Republic, Nicaragua, Honduras, Ecuador, El Salvador, Bolivia, Peru, Honduras, Colombia, Spain, Cuba, Guatemala, Argentina, Puerto Rico, Chile, Uruguay, Panama, and Paraguay.

OTHER LANGUAGES

Space limitations preclude a full look at all the ethnic and immigrant groups contributing to the state's linguistic diversity. Such extended treatment would include Basque immigrants (who settled in eastern Oregon from about the late nineteenth century to about 1940); Finns (who settled in Astoria); French and French Canadians; Germans, Dutch, and Swiss; Swedes and Norwegians throughout the region, but famously in the Seattle neighborhood of Ballard and the towns of Poulsbo and Stanwood; Greeks in Portland; Roma; and numerous political refugees—Hmong, Vietnamese, Cambodian, Lao, Ethiopian, Sudanese, Somalian, Liberian, Congolese, Polish, Romanian, Ukrainian, and, most recently, Syrian.

In sum, linguistic diversity in the Pacific Northwest looks something like table 1.1, according to the Language Map Data Center of the Modern Language Association.[5]

URBANIZATION, TOURISM, AND TRANSPLANTS

Settlement, emigration, and immigration tell part of the story of language diversity, but other factors also bring speech varieties into contact and introduce new variation. The difficulties of early migration kept the Pacific Northwest relatively isolated compared with the US South and East, until the transcontinental railways were completed in 1883.

Reshaped in the twentieth century by the New Deal and World War II, the Pacific Northwest developed an infrastructure of highways (including highways I-5 and I-84, begun in 1957), dams, and universities. Logging and

Table 1.1. Language Profile for Oregon and Washington

Oregon			Washington		
English	3,021,536	85.63%	English	5,060,313	82.51%
All languages other than English combined	507,200	14.37%	All Languages other than English combined	1,073,002	17.49%
Spanish	304,631	8.63%	Spanish	477,566	7.79%
Vietnamese	24,163	0.68%	Vietnamese	57,895	0.94%
Russian	21,443	0.61%	Tagalog	51,301	0.84%
German	17,299	0.49%	Korean	50,757	0.83%
Chinese	15,742	0.45%	Russian	49,282	0.80%
Korean	11,233	0.32%	Chinese	46,445	0.76%
Japanese	11,222	0.32%	German	33,744	0.55%
French	10,611	0.30%	Japanese	23,884	0.39%
Tagalog	7,853	0.22%	French	20,039	0.33%
Arabic	6,209	0.18%	Ukrainian	16,674	0.27%
Romanian	5,180	0.15%	Mon-Khmer	13,399	0.22%
Ukrainian	4,711	0.13%	Cantonese	13,189	0.22%
Hindi	3,801	0.11%	Mandarin	12,918	0.21%
Other	34,377	0.97%	Other	122,156	1.99%

lumber manufacturing and associated industries dominated the economy, while fishing and canning declined. By the 1990s, however, the timber boom was ending and the economy of the Pacific Northwest was shifting again, in the direction of technology and tourism.

Emerging industries have been a draw for skilled workers in the Portland and Seattle metro areas in particular. The Portland area, Willamette Valley, and Southern and Central Oregon (Ashland, Medford, Bend, Jacksonville) have also been loci of tourism and emigrant retirees, bringing new language and dialect features to the state. One indicator of emigration from other states is the surrender of driver's licenses from other states; the *Atlas of Oregon* reports that the 1995–2000 annual average was 24,032 licenses turned in from California, 14,283 from Washington, and 3,220 from Arizona (Loy et al. 2001, 41). The speech of Oregon and Washington is changing, influenced by emigrants from its northern and southern neighbors—with Portland and Seattle sandwiched between changes coming from California and Canada (see Becker, this volume, and Wassink, this volume).

STUDYING LANGUAGE DIVERSITY IN THE PACIFIC NORTHWEST

The linguistic history of the Pacific Northwest is ripe for further exploration and documentation. The preceding discussion serves as a prolegomenon to research questions about the languages and linguistic diversity of the region. How do we study and read the language history of a region further? At a general level, we must ask what factors of geography, economics, politics, and culture were involved in settlement and language contact. How does the early linguistic history manifest itself over time through language change? What forces (such as exclusionism and assimilationism) impact most heavily on languages other than English, and how were (and how are) these forces both promulgated and resisted? There is much to explore.

Notes

1   *Cumtux* is the Chinuk Wawa term for 'to know', *ictas* means 'things or belongings', *muckamuck* means 'food', and *tillicum* means 'people' or 'family'. *The Dictionary of American Regional English* is also a resource. Between 1965 and 1970, DARE fieldworkers interviewed seventeen participants from various parts of Oregon, and DARE indexes eighteen forms as related to the state, including *cho cho* (labelled OR), *cobra plant* (labeled nCA, swOR), *doghole* (nCA, sOR coasts), *jota* (esp CA, sID, eO), and *wheat duck* (OR) and *wokas* (chiefly sOR, nCA).

2   The town of French Prairie, for example, was settled by bicultural French Canadian and Indian families in the 1830s (see Jetté 2004).

3   The Old Believers or *starovery* split the Russian Orthodox Church in the seventeenth century, rejecting a set of reforms instituted by the patriarch (see Humphrey 2014).

4   The Page Act excluded anyone from "China, Japan, or any Oriental country . . . for lewd and immoral purposes," in its implementation preventing the entry of potential wives for Chinese men (see Chang 2004).

5   The MLA Language Map Data Center provides information about more than three hundred languages spoken in the United States, using data from the American Community Survey and the 2000 US Census (see https:// apps.mla.org/map_data).

References

Adams, D. W. 1995. *Education for Extinction: American Indians and the Boarding School Experience, 1875–1928.* Lawrence: University Press of Kansas.

Allen, C. 2004. "Filipinos Want Equal Rights or Independence." *Oregon History Project.* Portland: Oregon Historical Society. http://oregonhistoryproject. org/articles/historical-records/filipinos-want-equal-rights-or-independence/#.V1gi4mcUUdU.

Arima, E. Y. 1983. *The West Coast Nootka People.* Victoria: British Columbia Provincial Museum.

Barman, J., and B. Watson. 2006. *Leaving Paradise: Indigenous Hawaiians in the Pacific Northwest, 1787–1898. Honolulu:* University of Hawai'i Press.

Beckham, S. D., and R. B. Pamplin Jr. 2016. "Oregon History." *The Oregon Blue Book.* http://bluebook.state.or.us/cultural/history/history.htm.

Berg, L., ed. 2007. *The First Oregonians.* Corvallis: Oregon State University Press.

Bowen, W. A. 1978. *The Willamette Valley: Migration and Settlement on the Oregon Frontier.* Seattle: University of Washington Press.

Boyd, R. 1999. *The Coming of the Spirit of Pestilence: Introduced Infectious Diseases and Population Decline among Northwest Indians, 1774–1874.* Seattle: University of Washington Press.

Bussell, R., ed. 2008. *Understanding the Immigrant Experience in Oregon.* Eugene: University of Oregon. http://library.state.or.us/ repository/2008/200805231544055/index.pdf.

Carlton, C. R. 1934. "Hawaiians in Early Oregon." *Oregon Historical Quarterly* 35 (1): 22–31. Portland: Oregon Historical Society. http://www.jstor.org/ stable/20610848.

Center for the Study of the Pacific Northwest. n.d. "Industrialization, Class, and Race; Chinese and the Anti-Chinese Movement in the Late 19th-Century Northwest." Seattle: University of Washington. http://www. washington.edu/uwired/outreach/cspn/Website/Classroom%20Materials/ Pacific%20Northwest%20History/Lessons/Lesson%2015/15.html.

Chang, I. 2004. *The Chinese in America: A Narrative History.* New York: Penguin.

Collins, C. C. 1998. "Oregon's Carlisle: Teaching 'America' at Chemawa Indian School." *Columbia: The Magazine of Northwest History* 12 (2): 6–10.

Deur, D. 2011. "An Ethnohistorical Overview of Groups with Ties to Fort Vancouver National Historic Site." Seattle: University of Washington. http://depts.washington.edu/pnwcesu/reports/J9W88050025_Final_ Report.pdf.

Dictionary of American Regional English (DARE). 1985–2013. Edited by F. G. Cassidy and J. H. Hall. Cambridge, MA: Belknap Press/Harvard University Press.

Fixico, D. L. 2018. "Termination and Restoration in Oregon." *The Oregon Encyclopedia*. http://oregonencyclopedia.org/articles/termination_and_restoration/#.V1b8u2cUUdV.

Fixico, D. L. 1986. *Termination and Relocation: Federal Indian Policy, 1945–1960*. Albuquerque: University of New Mexico Press.

Gamboa, E., and C. M. Baun, eds. 1995. *Nosotros: The Hispanic People of Oregon*. Portland: Oregon Council for the Humanities.

Garcia, J. 2018. "Latinos in Oregon." *The Oregon Encyclopedia*. https://oregonencyclopedia.org/articles/hispanics_in_oregon/#.XD4vtM17kaE.

Governor's Office of Indian Affairs. 2016. Washington State Tribal Directory. http://www.goia.wa.gov/tribal-directory/tribaldirectory.pdf.

Gross, J., ed. 2007. *Teaching Oregon Native Languages*. Corvallis: Oregon State University Press.

Guzman, G. 2006. "Latino History of Washington State." http://www.HistoryLink.org.

Hoover, A. L., ed. 2002. *Nuu-Chah-Nulth Voices: Histories, Objects and Journeys*. Victoria: Royal British Columbia Museum.

Humphrey, C. 2014. "Schism, Event, and Revolution: The Old Believers of Trans-Baikalia." *Current Anthropology* 55 (S10): S216–S225.

Jetté, M. 2004. At the Hearth of the Crossed Races: Intercultural Relations and Social Change in French Prairie, Oregon, 1812–1843. PhD diss., University of British Columbia, Vancouver.

Katagiri, G. 2018. "Japanese Americans in Oregon." *The Oregon Encyclopedia*. http://oregonencyclopedia.org/articles/japanese_americans_in_oregon_immigrants_from_the_west/#.V1QeamcUUdV.

Knipe, Rev. C. 1868. *Some account of the Tahkaht language, as spoken by several tribes on the western coast of Vancouver island*. London: Hatchard.

Lang, G. 2008. *Making Wawa: The Genesis of Chinook Jargon*. Vancouver: University of British Columbia Press.

Lee, D. 2018. "Chinese Americans in Oregon." *The Oregon Encyclopedia*. https://oregonencyclopedia.org/articles/chinese_americans_in_oregon/#.V91MbWcUXcs.

Lewis. D. G. 2009. Termination of the Confederated Tribes of the Grand Ronde Community of Oregon: Politics, Community, Identity. PhD diss., University of Oregon, Eugene. https://scholarsbank.uoregon.edu/xmli/handle/1794/10067.

Loy, W. G., S. Allan, J. E. Meacham, and A. R. Buckley. 2001. *Atlas of Oregon*. Eugene: University of Oregon Press.

McLagan, E. 1980. *Peculiar Paradise: A History of Blacks in Oregon, 1788–1940*. Athens, GA: Georgian Press.

Millner, D. 2018. "Blacks in Oregon." *The Oregon Encyclopedia*. http://oregonencyclopedia.org/articles/blacks_in_oregon/#.V1gaX2cUUdU.

Millner, D. 1995. "George Bush of Tumwater: Founder of the First American Colony on Puget Sound." *Columbia Magazine* 8 (4): 14–19.

Mills, R. V. 1950. "Oregon Speechways." *American Speech* 25 (2): 81–90.

Modern Language Association. n.d. *The MLA Language Map Data Center.* https://apps.mla.org/map_data/.

Motel, S., and E. Patton. 2013. "Statistical Portrait of Hispanics in the United States, 2011." Pew Research Center Hispanic Trends. http://www.pewhispanic.org/2013/02/15/statistical-portrait-of-hispanics-in-the-united-states-2011/.

Nonato, J. 2016. Finding Manilatown: The Search for Seattle's Filipino American Community, 1898–2016. History Undergraduate Theses, Paper 24. http://digitalcommons.tacoma.uw.edu/cgi/viewcontent.cgi?article=1024&context=history_theses.

Office of Refugee Resettlement. Refugee Arrival Data. 2015. https://www.acf.hhs.gov/orr/resource/fy-2015-served-populations-by-state-and-country-of-origin-refugees-only.

Osipovich, T. n.d. "Russian Speaking Communities in Oregon." Portland: Lewis and Clark College. https://sites.google.com/a/lclark.edu/rsco/.

Robbins, W. G. 2018. "Oregon Donation Land Act." *The Oregon Encyclopedia.* http://www.oregonencyclopedia.org/articles/oregon_donation_land_act/#.V0mu5GcUUdU.

Strandjord, C. 2009. "Filipino Resistance to Anti-Miscegenation Laws in Washington State." The Great Depression in Washington State Project. http://depts.washington.edu/depress/filipino_anti_miscegenation.shtml.

Suttles, W. 1987. *Coast Salish Essays.* Seattle: University of Washington Press.

Taylor, Q. 1998. "'There Was No Better Place to Go': The Transformation Thesis Revisited, African American Migration to the Pacific Northwest, 1940–1950." In *Terra Pacific: People and Place in Northwest America and Western Canada*, edited by P. Hirt. Pullman: Washington State University Press.

University of Washington. 2009. "Mapping and Enhancing Language Learning in Washington State." http://depts.washington.edu/mellwa/index.php.

US Census Bureau. 2015. "American Community Survey, 2010 American Community Survey Table 38: Detailed Languages Spoken at Home. Ability to Speak English for the Population 5 Years and Over for Oregon: 2009–2013." https://www.census.gov/data/tables/2013/demo/2009-2013-lang-tables.html.

Wong, M. R. 2004. *Sweet Cakes, Long Journey: The Chinatowns of Portland, Oregon.* Seattle: University of Washington Press.

2

Place-Names of the Pacific Northwest

ALLAN RICHARDSON

> "Ish River"—
>> like breath,
>> like mist rising from a hillside.
> Duwamish, Snohomish, Stillaguamish, Samish,
> Skokomish, Skykomish . . . all the ish rivers.
>
> I live in Ish River country
> between two mountain ranges where
> many rivers
> run down to an inland sea.
>
> Robert Sund (2004, 1)

Place-names are an important part of the distinctive vocabulary of the Pacific Northwest today and provide a valuable record of the history of the region. In broad terms, place-names are embedded in cultural traditions and give fascinating insights to Indigenous cultures and early traditions in Europe. For example, the place-name "Oxford" is clearly 'ox-ford' and names a location where oxen were able to ford or cross a small river in England. Native Indigenous names in the Pacific Northwest often have similar practical meanings, while many other Native place-names have ties to mythical stories. In contrast to either of these sources of meaning, English place-names in the Pacific Northwest are labels recently given to objects. A sense of tradition and a relationship to the land have developed among the descendants of the settlers and immigrants to this area, as evidenced by their attachment to the names of the cities, rivers, and other places. People also identify with regions such as "ish river country" and "Cascadia." Although the origins of the place-names are quite different than in the Native languages, and the relationship to the land is very different, the naming of places gives speakers of English in the Northwest a sense of place. Before exploring the origins of place-names used in the Pacific Northwest today, let us look further at how the Native peoples of the Pacific Northwest used place-names as part of their relationship to the land.

Native American peoples had detailed knowledge of the land, much of which was expressed in place-names. The contrast with the non-Native view is emphasized by Eugene Hunn (1990):

> Columbia River Indians also named hundreds of specific places. Their ethnogeography differs systematically from the Euro-American in certain telling ways; for example, they did not usually name mountains and rivers as such. For non-Indians, a focus in specific mountain and rivers as things of importance implies a cartographic perspective, one in which the observer is placed above the landscape as if in flight. The Indians' land-based perspective named instead specific places on a mountain or along a river *where things happened*. It was a practical rather than a purely abstract geography, naming culturally significant places, the sites of important events or activities, whether of the present or of the myth age. (93)

The naming of places based on their importance in peoples' lives is demonstrated by Richardson and Galloway in their study of Nooksack place-names. They found that the largest number of places were named for environmental features (such as 'always has a lake', 'clear water', 'rocky bottom creek'), with the next largest group named for plants or animals ('black hawthorn berry', 'tall marsh blueberry plant', 'spring salmon place', 'always butter clams'), most of which were food sources (2011, 193–194). "The knowledge of flora and fauna used for food, so important for survival, is preserved in place names. Naming places after some environmental factors also has survival value, as does naming them for descriptive orientation, especially when someone is lost or needs to confirm his or her location" (Richardson and Galloway 2011, 211). Further connections to the land are shown in the many places named after activities of the Nooksack people ('crossing,' 'trading,' 'resting,' 'shooting') that took place at specific locations. In addition to practical need, for Native people, place-names are part of a spiritual relationship to the land. This is expressed in the *Sahaptian Place Names Atlas* (Hunn et al. 2015) as follows:

> Many land forms and features on the land are explained by an event narrated in our myths. In each story, there is a link to the landscape that ties the story to the place and can be passed on to the next generation. Children, in learning place names, learn to recognize features of the landscape by their form, their meanings in the oral literature, and their ecological significance. One example of a geographically visual myth is about Abalone Girl's tears, a place located south of *Táptat* (Prosser, Washington) in the vicinity of an important Indian trail. . . . As she walked along toward her home, she cried. Her tears fell and splashed down the side of the ridge above *Táptat.* Today, these tears are still there, reflected as talus markings on the hill. (27–28)

Many of the places named in myths can be termed transformer sites, where a person or animal was turned to stone (or another landform) by a supernatural being. Throughout the Pacific Northwest many hundreds, likely thousands, of place-names were similarly embodied in traditional myths and legends. The Native peoples lived in a landscape that was an expression of their belief systems and provided for their survival needs. The use of some of these place-names in the speech of non-Indigenous people no longer has the religious or practical connection of the original, yet it does give a distinctive quality to modern-day English in the Pacific Northwest.

Indigenous-derived names are in wide use today for many geographic features, and for numerous cities, towns, and counties in the Pacific Northwest. These names give recognition to Native peoples but are removed from Native context, and original meanings are lost, or obscured by erroneous etymologies. As a prime example, the ways in which the city of Seattle has mythologized its Native namesake and exploited its Native identity are explored at length by Coll Thrush in his book *Native Seattle* (Thrush 2007). A more positive romanticizing of place-names with Native roots occurs with the concept of "ish river country," a view of the Puget Sound region popularized by poets and other writers, notably Robert

Sund. What is the source of the names of the "ish" rivers, and the many other Native-sounding river names? How are these and other Native-origin place-names linked to actual words in Native languages?

The names used today for most of the rivers in our region come from Native languages, yet few of these were used as river names by the Native people. The "ish" rivers of Western Washington were all named by English speakers taking forms ending with the Lushootseed suffix -amish or -mish (-abš, -bš) meaning 'people.' These rivers were named for groups of people living on the rivers: "Thus stùləgʷábš 'river people', from stúləkʷ 'river', became Stillaguamish, and sqʼíxʷəbš 'upstream people', from sqʼíxʷ 'upstream', became Skykomish" (Suttles and Lane 1990, 501). Puyallup has a similar origin in puyáləpabš, meaning "people of the bend because their river is full of bends" (Bates, Hess, and Hilbert 1994, 165), but the -abš ending was not included. The name for the Nooksack River comes from the name of an important site on the river, Nexwsá7aq nuxʷsǽ7æq 'always bracken fern roots' (Richardson and Galloway 2011, 111). A mistaken etymology for Nooksack includes "Noot-saak, meaning 'fern-eating people.' (*Noot*—'people'; *Saak*—'bracken fern')" (Hitchman 1985, 210). The Willamette River and Falls were named after wálamt, a village located below Willamette Falls (Lewis, Thorsgard, and Williams 2013, 310). Eugene Hunn (1991) generalizes this pattern:

> The Native names now assigned to many Northwest rivers referred in the original languages to major villages or fishing sites on those rivers. **Táytin** (Tieton) named a spear-fishing site at the outlet of Clear Lake high up the Tieton River. In Sahaptin, **łátaxat** (Klickitat) named the key Klickitat River fishery at the falls just above the river's mouth. **Iyákima** (Yakima), literally "the pregnant ones," indicated a string of hills near the present-day city of Yakima named for their resemblance to five pregnant women of a mythological account. (170)

Schuster (1998, 348) provides a different etymology for Yakima in *yákama* 'black bears', but gives the earliest historic form from 1811 as Eyakima, which supports the other origin for the name. The Native people now refer to themselves as the Yakama Nation, while the spelling Yakima continues in use for the city, county, river, and valley. Two additional Native-origin river names with extended uses are Walla Walla and Palouse. Walla

Walla comes from Sahaptin *walawála* 'many small streams.' "The name refers to the Walla Walla valley, which is bisected by numerous streams" (Hunn et al. 2015, 96). The name Palouse, used for the region, town, and river in Eastern Washington, comes from the name of the Palouse Indian village (usually spelled Palus) located at the mouth of the Palouse River. "The village name comes directly from Sahaptin *palúus* (Palouse dialect *pelúus*, literally 'what is standing up in the water'). . . . The name appears to be a reference to a large rock in the center of the Snake River just upriver from the mouth of the Palouse River" (Sprague 1998, 358).

The "Native flavor" to modern Northwest geography includes more than the many river names, as in the cases of Tillamook, Klamath, Chinook, Multnomah, and Whatcom. Tillamook is a bay on the Oregon coast made famous for its creamery. "The name Tillamook derives from Chinookan tʔilimuks 'those of niʔilim'; the etymology of the place-name . . . is unknown" (Seaburg and Miller 1990, 566). Klamath is the name of a lake and a river, and the basis of the name for the city of Klamath Falls. "The name Klamath is a borrowing from Upper Chinookan ɬámaɬ, literally 'they of the river, they who have a river,' a designation derived from the stem -maɬ 'river'" (Stern 1998, 464). Although these two place-names come from Chinookan languages, the name Chinook does not:

> The name "Chinook" (pronounced with "ch" as in "chin" not "shin") is from c'inúk, the Lower Chehalis name for a village on Baker Bay, in the Columbia River estuary, and for its inhabitants. Early Euro-Americans adopted the name for the people who lived around the mouth of the Columbia and in time extended it to include all those who spoke the languages that are now recognized as members of the Chinookan language family. (Boyd, Ames, and Johnson 2013, x)

Chinook today names a town in Washington State near the original location. Multnomah, the county that includes Portland, Oregon, was originally a village name: "Multnomah is from máɬnumax̣ 'those toward the water' ('those closer to the Columbia River'). The spelling Mult-no-mah appears already in Lewis and Clark" (Silverstein 1990, 545). Whatcom, the county that includes Bellingham, Washington, began as the Native name for Whatcom Creek and the camp at the mouth of Whatcom Creek. In the Nooksack language it is X̱wó̱tqwem x̣ʷátqʷəm 'sound of water splashing or dripping fast and hard' (Richardson and Galloway 2011, 173). The same name is used in the Lummi language, and it was the Lummi who directed early settlers to this location, where they founded the town of Whatcom. The name is often said to mean 'noisy waters,' which is close to the original meaning.

Perhaps the most prominent of all place-names with Native American origins are the names of the three largest cities of Washington State: Seattle, Spokane, and Tacoma. The name Spokane—*spoqíni* 'round-head,' for the Native people living on the Spokane River—was recorded by David Thompson as early as 1810, the same year that Spokane House was established by the North West Company on the Spokane River downstream from the modern city (Ross 1998, 280–281). Popular place-name books assert that the name Spokane refers to the sun, for example: "This name appears to be from the Indian tribal designation, *Spehkunne,* meaning 'Children of the Sun' or 'Sun People'" (Hitchman 1985, 285). Following either etymology, the name of the city of Spokane comes from the name of a Native group, the Spokane Indians. The name Tacoma comes from the Native name for the dominant mountain peak of the region, known in English as Mount Rainier. The Lushootseed word təqʷúbəʔ 'permanently snow-covered mountain' was used by people in the southern parts of Puget Sound to name Mount Rainier (Bates, Hess, and Hilbert 1994, 223). Since "b" was often heard as "m," Tacoma is a close approximation of the Native name for the mountain that overlooks the modern city. In contrast to other Native-origin place-names, Seattle is named after a Native individual, known to English speakers as Chief Seattle. The plat for the town of Seattle was filed in May 1853.

> Although the Whulshootseed name for the site was now familiar to many of the settlers, the "awkward and meaningless" word meaning Little Crossing-Over Place was never considered as a name for the town, while Duamps and Duwamish River, two other options used briefly during 1852, were considered ugly and unflattering. Instead, the community leaders chose to name their town after Seeathl. (Thrush 2007, 37)

The city's namesake was Siʔaɫ Chief Seattle (Bates, Hess, and Hilbert 1994, 380), one of the leaders of the Duwamish and Suquamish peoples who was especially helpful to the pioneer settlers. Interestingly, the Indigenous native speakers of Lushootseed continued to use the name sdZéédZul7aleecH dᶻidᶻəlal'ič Little Crossing-Over Place (lit. 'little crossing of the back') for Seattle for another hundred years after its founding (Thrush 2007, 229–230; Bates, Hess, and Hilbert 1994, 91). Before the naming of Seattle and other early settler towns, a great many geographic places in the Pacific Northwest were named by European and Euro-American explorers and fur traders.

The earliest definite naming of places in the Pacific Northwest by non-Natives was in 1775 by Spanish maritime explorer Bruno Heceta. He gave the name Cabo San Roque to the point now known as Cape Disappointment, just north of the mouth of the Columbia River, and "noted the indications of a river there" (McArthur 1992, 195). Heceta also named a point of land Cabo Falcon, but not necessarily the same point in the Tillamook area that bears the name Cape Falcon today. Heceta was remembered by later mapmakers in the naming of Heceta Head. The name Cape Blanco, for the westernmost point of land in Oregon, recognizes a much earlier Spanish expedition in 1602–1603 under Vizcaino. One of his boats captained by Martin de Aguilar named Cape Blanco at a claimed latitude of 43 degrees North. It is unlikely that de Aguilar was that far north, but later mapmakers gave the name Cape Blanco to the prominent point at that latitude (McArthur 1992, 139–140).

In the late eighteenth century the Spanish and British empires were competing for influence on the Northwest Coast, and the next naming of places was by James Cook in 1778. The first two places that Cook named in his voyage to the north Pacific Coast were Cape Foulweather and Cape Perpetua, both on March 7, 1778. The weather was foul, and it was St. Perpetua's Day, honoring Perpetua the Martyr, who died on this date in the year 203 (McArthur 1992, 144). Another name that comes from Captain Cook is Cape Flattery, but the location he named is uncertain. The name was placed where it is now in 1792 by George Vancouver, who was a member of Cook's crew in 1778 (Meany 1923, 35). Another coastal landmark has what may be the oldest English name at its original location in Washington State: Cape Disappointment, named by English explorer John Meares in 1788 while searching for the river mouth reported by Heceta (Meany 1923, 35). Meares also named Mount Olympus (Meany 1923, 177), and named the Strait of Juan de Fuca after its supposed original discoverer, who claimed to have explored the area in 1592 (Meany 1923, 291–292).

Many Spanish names for islands and waterways in Washington State come from explorations by Manuel Quimper in 1790 and Francisco de

Eliza in 1791. Four prominent Washington place-names can be traced to the Quimper expedition, but just one of these is even part of the same name for the same place. On the outer coast Quimper named an inlet Boca de Alava, with the name transferred to Cape Alava much later. In the inland waters he gave the name Ensenada de Caamaño to what is now Admiralty Inlet, Boca de Fidalgo to the opening of the present Rosario Strait, and Canal de Lopez de Haro to Haro Strait (see map 113 in Hayes 1999, 71). Camano Island and Fidalgo Island were not recognized as islands by the early explorers, receiving their names in the nineteenth century, prior to 1841 (see map 101 in Hayes 2011, 44). The name Canal de Lopez de Haro was modified by Vancouver to Canal de Arro, then restored to its Spanish spelling as Haro Strait by later mapmakers (see map 101 in Hayes 2011, 44).

A map from the Eliza expedition of 1791 (see map 117 in Hayes 1999, 73) includes the following places: Isla y Archipielago de San Juan, Boca de Orcasitas, Canal de Fidalgo, Seno de Padilla, Isla de Güemes, Isla Sucia, Isla de Patos, Gran Canal de Nuestra Señora del Rosario, and Puerto de Nuestra Señora de los Angeles. Three of these come from parts of the name of the viceroy of New Spain, Juan Vicente de Güemes Padilla Horcasitas y Aguayo. The San Juan Islands, Padilla Bay, Guemes Island, Sucia Island, and Patos Island have kept the names given by Eliza. Boca de Orcasitas was given to the southern opening of present-day San Juan Channel and is the source of the name for Orcas Island (Meany, 1923, pp. 200–201). The Gran Canal de Nuestra Señora del Rosario was the first European name for today's Georgia Strait, whereas Canal de Fidalgo named today's Rosario Strait. Vancouver includes both as part of his Gulph of Georgia, named in honor of King George III (see maps 150 and 153 in Hayes 1999, 92–93). The name Rosario Strait was placed at its current location some time prior to 1841 (see map 101 in Hayes 2011, 44). Puerto de Nuestra Señora de los Angeles was simplified to Puerto de los Angeles in 1792, and later Anglicized to Port Angeles.

In 1792, the explorers Galiano and Valdes (Spanish), Vancouver (British), and Gray (American) explored and named places in the Northwest. Galiano and Valdes began in the Strait of Juan de Fuca, then explored northward, giving new names to places now in Canada. Vancouver became the first European to explore the Puget Sound region, giving many of the place-names that we still use for its waterways, islands, and mountains. Gray explored along the outer coast and is famous for the discovery and naming of the Columbia River: "Captain Robert Gray, in the

American vessel *Columbia*, on May 11, 1792, at 8 A.M., sailed through the breakers and at 1 P.M. anchored in the river ten miles from its mouth. On May 19, Captain Gray gave his ship's name to the river" (Meany 1923, 52). Gray also discovered Grays Harbor, which he named Bulfinch Harbor, which was then named Gray's Harbor by George Vancouver later in 1792 (Meany 1923, 102). For his own discoveries, Vancouver used the names of English aristocrats connected to the Royal Navy, other naval officers, and members of his own crew, as well as descriptions of local geography. Point Grenville south of the mouth of the Quinault River is named for Lord Grenville, who became secretary of foreign affairs in 1791 (Meany 1957, 64); Port Townshend (now Port Townsend) in honor of the Marquis Townshend (Meany 1957, 95); Bellingham's Bay for Sir William Bellingham, whose "office was controller of the storekeeper's accounts of his Majesty's Navy" (Meany 1957, 209); Hood's Channel (now Hood Canal) for the Right Honorable Lord Hood, a member of the Board of Admiralty (Meany 1957, 109–111); a few months later, Mount Hood was also named in his honor. Three fellow naval officers were honored in the naming of Vashon's Island, "after my friend Captain Vashon of the navy"; Mount Rainier after "my friend Rear Admiral Rainier"; and Point Roberts "after my esteemed friend and predecessor in the *Discovery*" (Meany 1957, 145, 99, 182–183). Three prominent landmarks of Western Washington were named for members of Vancouver's crew: Mount Baker was named for Third Lieutenant Joseph Baker, who was the first to sight this peak (Meany 1957, 81–82); Lieutenant Peter Puget was honored by the name Puget's Sound, originally just the southernmost inland waters of Western Washington, but historically and today extended far to the north (Meany 1957, 147–148); and Whidbey's Island was named for Joseph Whidbey, the first to circumnavigate his namesake island (Meany 1957, 178). Deception Passage (now Deception Pass) was named such because of its narrow and difficult channel, Cypress Island likely for an abundance of juniper trees, and Birch Bay for birch trees. After 1792, most of the exploration and naming of places in the Northwest shifts inland, with the exception of the Wilkes Expedition in 1841.

The United States Exploring Expedition (U.S. Ex. Ex.), led by Commander Charles Wilkes, departed for the southern oceans in 1838 and spent much of 1841 on the Northwest Coast. In the inland waters of Western Washington, many of the smaller islands were given European names for the first time, and many previously named places were given new English names to replace those given by the Spanish explorers. The San Juan

Islands were renamed the Navy Archipelago, described as "a collection of 25 islands having the Straits of Fuca on the south, the Gulf of Georgia on the north, the Canal de Arro on the west, and Ringgold's Channel on the east. They have been named for distinguished officers late of the US Naval service, viz., Rodgers, Chauncey, Hull, Shaw, Decatur, Jones, Blakely, Perry, Sinclair, Lawrence, Gordon, Percival, and others" (quoted in Meany 1923, 183). Rodgers, Chauncey, and Hull are better known as San Juan, Lopez, and Orcas Islands; San Juan as the largest island of the San Juan archipelago; Lopez taken from Canal de Lopez de Haro; and Orcas from Orcasitas, as stated earlier (Meany 1923, 150–151, 256). Shaw, Decatur, Jones, Blakely, and Sinclair are among the many names from the U.S. Ex. Ex. still in use. Perhaps the most unusual name given by the Wilkes expedition is Vendovi Island, named for a Fijian chief being taken back to the United States as a prisoner (Meany 1923, 327; Blumenthal 2012, 266).

Several land-based ventures named places in the Northwest early in the nineteenth century. The Lewis and Clark Expedition arrived in the Northwest in 1805 and returned east in 1806. Soon after a difficult portage around the Cascades Rapids they named Beacon Rock on the north bank, written as "Beaten Rock" on Clark's field map, and the Quicksand River, changed to Sandy River by later settlers, entering from the south (Beckham 2002, 57–59). On the return trip the following spring they named Mount Jefferson for the American president (McArthur 1992, 591). Lewis and Clark had spent the winter on the south shore of the mouth of the Columbia River near present-day Astoria, Oregon. The first American settlement on the Pacific Coast was established here in 1811 by the Pacific Fur Company and named Astoria for its owner, J. J. Astor (McArthur 1992, 30). The John Day River in eastern Oregon was named for Astor employee John Day, who was attacked, then rescued on the Columbia River near the mouth of his namesake river in 1812 (McArthur 1992, 451–452). British fur companies employing many French Canadians led to a number of place-names with French origins, notably The Dalles, Grande Ronde Valley, and Deschutes River, all in Oregon, and the Pend Oreille River in northeast Washington. The original French forms of these were all in use by the 1820s: *dalles,* referring to flat stones, named the narrow rapids in the Columbia close by the modern city of The Dalles (McArthur 1992, 826–827); *grande ronde* named the round valley in northeastern Oregon, with the name extended to the Grande Ronde River and the city of La Grande (McArthur 1992, 371); *Riviere des Chutes* was named for the falls on the Columbia River near the mouth of the Deschutes River (McArthur 1992, 249–250). The much smaller Deschutes River in Washington State was named for the falls in the river at a location later known as Tumwater, Chinook Jargon for waterfall (Meany 1923, 318; Thomas 1970, 101). *pend d'oreille,* meaning 'ear-drop' or 'earbob,' was the name given to the Native people living along this river (Lahren 1998, 296). The name given to the Nez Perce people, from the French *nez percé* 'pierced nose,' has a similar origin. The Rogue River in southern Oregon was first named in French *La Riviere aux Coquins,* and later given the English translation as the Rogue River (McArthur 1992, 719–720). The fur companies also employed many Hawaiians, which resulted in several Hawaiian place-names in this region (see chapter 1).

Three other important place-names gradually came into use in the early nineteenth century: Cascade Mountains, Oregon, and Snake River. Early explorers such as Lewis and Clark use phrases such as "Western mountains covered with snow" to describe the Cascades. David Douglas, the botanist, uses "Cascade Mountains" in his journals written in 1823–1827, which is the earliest documented use of the phrase that we use today (McArthur 1992, 152). The name Oregon was not used for a land area by any of the early explorers, fur traders, or mapmakers, gaining this use only after it was included in a volume of poetry published in 1817 (McArthur 1992, 637–640). Prior to this, variations of the word Oregon were used to name a river.

> The place name *Oregon* first appeared in literature in 1778 when Jonathan Carver published *Travels through the Interior Part of North America,* a book widely read in England and the United States. Carver reported Indian accounts of a great river in the Northwest known as the River Oregon. Soon *Oregon* appeared on published maps of the western continent, in some cases as a name for the river we know today as the Columbia. (Bryam and Lewis 2001, 128)

Carver's source for the name Oregon was the writings of Robert Rogers, a British officer in the upper Great Lakes region in the 1760s. It was Rogers who learned of a river route to the Pacific Ocean from Cree Indian traders. In Rogers's writings and maps the river name is usually spelled "Ourigan" and most likely applied to the Fraser River, which was part of a known northern trade route (Bryam and Lewis 2001, 128–129). Bryam and Lewis present the intriguing possibility that the word *ourigan* is derived from *ooligan,* one of the many names for the eulachon or candle-fish, whose oil was an important food source and trade commodity on the Northwest Coast and into the interior (2001, 130–134). The Snake River was first named by outsiders as the Lewis River by William Clark in honor of Meriwether Lewis, with the name Snake River first appearing in fur traders journals in the 1820s (Meany 1923, 278–279). The maps prepared following the Lewis and Clark Expedition include the "Shoshones or Snake Indians" living near the Lewis River (Beckham 2002, inside front cover). The use of "Snake Indians" for the Shoshones was well established. Hyde states in the last decades of the eighteenth century "in the Wyoming plains were the Gens du Serpent or Snakes, close relatives of the Comanches" and refers to "the great Gens du Serpent tribe of the period 1740–70" (Hyde 1974, 145). It is not clear why the Shoshones were called the "snake people," but they are remembered this way in the name of a great river.

Another important source of place-names with roots in the fur trade era is the Chinook Jargon, or Chinuk Wawa (this pidgin trade language is covered in detail in chapter 4). Place-names from this language include Wapato, Camas, Tumwater (described above), Cultus Lake, and the Pilchuck and Skookumchuck Rivers. *Wappato* in Chinook Jargon can refer to either potato or the native wapato (an edible aquatic tuber). Lewis and Clark's map includes Wappatoo Valley for the region surrounding the confluence of the Willamette and Columbia Rivers (Beckham 2002, inside front cover). This usage continues today, at least among academic professionals, who write about the Wapato Valley as an area rich in food resources, especially wapato, and with a notably dense Native population prior to the early historic disease epidemics (Gahr 2013, 69; Ellis 2013, 47). The city of Wapato near Yakima, Washington, also takes its name from the Chinook Jargon word. *Camas,* or *lakamas* 'camas root' is clearly the source of the name for the city of Camas, Washington, in early years known as La Camas (Meany 1923, 33–34). The origin of the word *camas* is from the Nez Perce language, with *lakamas* coming into Chinook Jargon through French (Lang 2008, 95). Gene Hunn discusses the word origins further: "Like cous, camas is named in both English and Latin, *Camassia quamash,* after the Cayuse Nez Perce term qéʔmʼes. . . . Meriwether Lewis collected the first modern scientific specimens of both cous and camas while passing through Nez Perce country and no doubt was taught the local names by his Nez Perce guides" (Hunn et al. 2015, 44). *Cultus* can mean "worthless, good for nothing, without purpose, bad, dissolute, filthy, foul, useless, worn out, damaged beyond repair, and also a degree of worthlessness which cannot be expressed in ordinary English" (Thomas 1970, 62). It is not clear why Cultus Lake, located near Bend, Oregon, received this name. *Pilchuck* means 'red water' and *Skookumchuck* means 'a powerful stream' (Thomas 1970, 61, 92). Pilchuck now names a river, a creek, a mountain, and a world-famous glass-blowing studio, all in Snohomish County, Washington. Skookumchuck River is a tributary of the Chehalis River in southwest Washington.

During the fur trade era, the Northwest was jointly occupied and used by the British and the Americans. Following the boundary settlement of 1846, an increasing flow of Americans came to live in the Pacific Northwest. More natural features and the new settlements received names from everyday English, American cities and towns in the East, American political figures, and the names of the settlers themselves. Thus we have the Three Sisters mountains and Crater Lake in Oregon, Twin Sisters Mountain and Glacier Peak in Washington, and innumerable place-names that include bear, deer, maple, and cedar. Albany, Oregon, was named for Albany, New York; Portland, Oregon, was named for Portland, Maine; Salem, Oregon, was named for Salem, Massachusetts (McArthur 1992, 8–9, 683, 734–735). Centralia, Washington, was named for Centralia, Illinois; Mount Vernon, Washington, was named for the Virginia home of George Washington (Meany 1923, 42, 180). American presidents were honored in the naming of the State of Washington, Lake Washington, Mount Adams, Jackson County and Jacksonville, and Lincoln County and Lincoln City. Lesser national political figures were used in naming Dallas, Oregon, for George Mifflin Dallas, vice president of the United States from 1845 to 1849, and Pendleton, Oregon, for the Democratic candidate for vice president in 1864 (McArthur 1992, 234–235, 659). Similarly, Blaine, Washington, was named for James G. Blaine, the Republican nominee for president in 1884 (Meany 1923, 21–22). In Oregon, Eugene was named for Eugene F. Skinner, the first settler at the location of the future city; Keizer was named for T. D. and J. B. Keizer, early pioneers who settled in the area where the town of Keizer started later; Roseburg was named for Aaron Rose, who settled on the site (McArthur 1992, 299, 463, 723). In Washington, Bremerton was named for city founder William Bremer; Ellensburg was named for Mary Ellen Shoudy, the wife of the city founder; and Anacortes is based on Anna

Curtis, the maiden name of the wife of the city founder (Meany 1923, 27, 78, 7). The unusual name of Sedro-Woolley, Washington, comes from the names of two towns that merged: Sedro, based on the Spanish *cedro* 'cedar,' and Woolley, founded by Philip A. Woolley (Meany 1923, 264–265).

Adapting foreign, non-Native, words is yet another source of new place-names. This was clearly the case in Sedro and was also involved in the naming of the towns of Corvallis and Estacada in Oregon: Corvallis was invented by the town founder "by compounding Latin words meaning heart of the valley" (McArthur 1992, 207); Estacada was chosen by a town founder who "selected the name at random from a map of the United States which showed *Llano Estacado,* in Texas" (McArthur 1992, 296). A somewhat indirect use of foreign words happened with *mazama*, which names a town in Washington, a lake and meadow (Mazama Park) on the slopes of Mount Baker, and a mountain in Oregon. As detailed by William Bright (2004),

> The name refers to a prehistoric volcanic mountain, the caldera is now occupied by Crater Lake. It was named for the Mazamas, a mountaineering club in Portland, in 1896 (McArthur 1992). The word *mazama* was used at one time to refer to the mountain sheep; but it is a species name for the brocket deer, an animal native to Latin America. It is derived from Nahuatl (Aztecan) *mazame* 'deer' (pl.)', from *mazatl* 'a deer'. (274)

This indirect borrowing from Nahuatl is unusual, yet it highlights the diversity of the origins of place-names in the Pacific Northwest.

Another approach to naming places historically and in recent years is to use the names to attract settlers and visitors, using actual or invented English words. Seaside, Oregon, and Bellevue and Fairhaven, Washington, are good examples. The effort at civic promotion failed in the case of Fairhaven, which was absorbed into the city of Bellingham. Late-twentieth-century efforts at promotion led to the names of Ocean Shores, Washington, and Sunriver, Oregon. A positive image and a desire to attract settlers was clearly at work in the naming of Seattle, discussed above, and no doubt in many other cases. New real estate developments continue to follow this pattern, but names can be added or changed for other reasons. Salish Sea and Cascadia have been added to the local vocabulary out of a need to communicate about broader features of our region.

Salish Sea is a recently adopted name used to designate all of the inland coastal waters of Washington and southern British Columbia. Bert Webber, a professor at Western Washington University, took the lead in the effort to have this new place-name recognized:

> In 1989, Webber requested that the Washington State Board on Geographic Names officially name the body of water consisting of the Puget Sound, the Strait of Juan de Fuca, and the Strait of Georgia, the Salish Sea. The board declined, stating that the name did not have popular usage. The first official recognition of the name came in 2008 by the Coast Salish, the region's original inhabitants and those the name is intended to honor. In 2009, the Washington State Board on Geographic Names, the US Board on Geographic Names, the Geographic Names Board of Canada, and finally the Cabinet of the Province of British Columbia all approved Salish Sea as the name of the jewel of the Pacific Northwest. (Benedict and Gaydos 2015, xi)

The Native peoples of the region share an identity as Salish people, but the name Salish is not originally from this area. Salish is the name used by a Native group in western Montana: "In the Flathead-Spokane language the Flathead proper, the people who were in the Bitterroot Valley in the nineteenth century, are called *séliš*" (Malouf 1998, 312). Based on many linguistic similarities, linguists and anthropologists use the name Salish for the language family that includes twenty-three languages formerly spoken over much of the Northwest Coast and interior, including the ten Central Coast Salish languages spoken around the Salish Sea.

In contrast to the Salish Sea, the area called Cascadia has no established boundaries, but varies according to the context. The Cascadia region affected by the Cascadia fault and its major earthquakes extends from Northern California to Vancouver Island and from the coast to the Cascade Mountains (Tucker 2015, 8). A more expansive view is taken by the author of *The People of Cascadia*, who posits the "'Lands of Cascadia' extend from southern Alaska to northern California and inland to the Continental Divide, encompassing all of those watershed which run into the Pacific Ocean" (Bohan 2009, 2). This definition is essentially the same as that shown for the Cascadia bioregion by the Cascadia Institute (McCloskey 2014). The northwest Washington *Cascadia Weekly* newspaper header states that it is "reporting from the heart of Cascadia." Cascadia may not be a specific site, but the concept does provide a sense of place to many residents of the Pacific Northwest.

What about place-names that people find objectionable? The names given to mountains are especially significant, as demonstrated in the renaming of Mount McKinley in Alaska to Denali in 2015:

> "This name change recognizes the sacred status of Denali to many Alaska Natives," Secretary Jewell said. "The name Denali has been official for use by the State of Alaska since 1975, but even more importantly, the mountain has been known as Denali for generations. With our own sense of reverence for this place, we are officially renaming the mountain Denali in recognition of the traditions of Alaska Natives and the strong support of the people of Alaska." (USGS 2015)

The names Mount Baker and Mount Rainier, given by Vancouver in 1792, have been contested at least as far back as the mid-nineteenth century. Theodore Winthrop, who visited the Northwest in 1853, wrote the following about the Cascade Range:

> Kulshan, misnamed Mount Baker by the vulgar, is their northernmost buttress . . . . Its name I got from the Lummi tribe at its base, after I had dipped in their pot at a boiled-salmon feast. As to Baker, that name should be forgotten. Mountains should not be insulted by being named after undistinguished bipeds. . . . South of Kulshan, the range continues dark, rough, and somewhat unmeaning to the eye, until it is relieved by Tacoma, *vulgo* Regnier. (Winthrop 1863, 47–48)

Although Kulshan is a close Anglicized approximation of the Lummi name for the mountain, it is not the name used by the Nooksack people who live closest to the mountain, so how would a Native name be chosen to replace Mount Baker? It is widely claimed that the Indian name for Mount Baker is "Koma Kulshan," but no such name is used for the mountain in any native language. The origin of this and other names for Mount Baker are explored in "Koma Kulshan: The Misnaming of a Mountain" (Richardson and Lloyd 2014). Civic leaders from the city of Tacoma, and Native groups more recently, have pushed to change the name of Mount Rainier to Tacoma or Tahoma, but any change is unlikely at this time because of the long-established and widespread usage of Rainier. In contrast, offensive place-names are being changed throughout the Northwest. Notable among the changes is the renaming of places including the term "squaw."

> In 2001, the Oregon State Legislature banned the use of the term "squaw" in Oregon place-names. While in its origin "squaw" was not a derogatory term, in Euro-American application it became insulting when used with ugly stereotypes, racial epithets, and demeaning images. The consequence is that 172 geographic names in Oregon may be replaced. In 2006, the CTUIR [Confederated Tribes of the Umatilla Indian Reservation] proposed ʔíšqúulktpe, a Cayuse Nez Perce word that translates to 'at the beheading/throat-cutting' to replace the word "squaw" in Squaw Creek, Little Squaw Creek, Squaw Creek Overlook, and Little Squaw Spring. . . . In 2007, the Oregon Geographic Names Board recommended approval of the change to the US Board of Geographic Names, which approved ʔíšqúulktpe for all four geographic names in 2008. (Hunn et al. 2015, 62–63)

Clearly place-names are a dynamic, not static, part of our language, even if many of them remain little changed for long spans of time.

Place-names matter to people in the Pacific Northwest. For the Native, Indigenous peoples, place-names frame their relationship to their traditional lands for both practical survival and spiritual sense of place. For the descendants of settlers and immigrants arriving here over the past two hundred years, place-names also provide a sense of place, but more in terms of ties to regions and communities. In all cases, place-names are an important and distinctive part of language spoken in the Pacific Northwest.

References

Bates, D., T. Hess, and V. Hilbert. 1994. *Lushootseed Dictionary.* Seattle: University of Washington Press.

Beckham, S. D. 2002. *Lewis and Clark from the Rockies to the Pacific.* Portland, OR: Graphic Arts Center Publishing.

Benedict, A. D., and J. K. Gaydos. 2015. *The Salish Sea*. Seattle, WA: Sasquatch Books.

Blumenthal, R. W. 2012. *Maritime Place Names: Inland Washington Waters*. Bellevue, WA: Inland Waters.

Bohan, H. 2009. *The People of Cascadia: Pacific Northwest Native American History*. Self-published.

Boyd, R. T., K. A. Ames, and T. A. Johnson, eds. 2013. *Chinookan Peoples of the Lower Columbia*. Seattle: University of Washington Press.

Bright, W. 2004. *Native American Placenames of the United States*. Norman: University of Oklahoma Press.

Bryam, S., and D. G. Lewis. 2001. "Ourigan: Wealth of the Northwest Coast." *Oregon Historical Quarterly* 102 (2): 126–157.

Ellis, D. V. 2013. "Cultural Geography of the Lower Columbia River." In *Chinookan Peoples of the Lower Columbia*, edited by R. T. Boyd, K. A. Ames, and T. A. Johnson, 42–62. Seattle: University of Washington Press.

Gahr, D. A. T. 2013. "Ethnobiology: Nonfishing Subsistence and Production." In *Chinookan Peoples of the Lower Columbia*, edited by R. T. Boyd, K. A. Ames, and T. A. Johnson, 63–79. Seattle: University of Washington Press.

Hayes, D. 1999. *Historical Atlas of the Pacific Northwest: Maps of Exploration and Discovery*. Seattle, WA: Sasquatch Books.

Hayes, D. 2011. *Historical Atlas of Washington and Oregon*. Berkeley: University of California Press.

Hitchman, R. 1985. *Place Names of Washington*. Tacoma: Washington State Historical Society.

Hunn, E. S. 1990. *Nch'i-Wána "The Big River": Mid-Columbia Indians and Their Land*. Seattle: University of Washington Press.

Hunn, E. S. 1991. Native Place Names on the Columbia Plateau. In *A Time of Gathering: Native Heritage in Washington State*, edited by R. K. Wright, 170–177. Seattle: University of Washington Press.

Hunn, E. S., E. T. Morning Owl, P. E. Cash, and J. Karson Engum. 2015. *Čáw Pawá Láakni: They Are Not Forgotten: Sahaptian Place Names Atlas of the Cayuse, Umatilla, and Walla Walla*. Pendleton, OR: Tamástslikt Cultural Institute.

Hyde, G. E. 1974. *The Pawnee Indians*. Norman: University of Oklahoma Press.

Lahren, S. L. Jr. 1998. "Kalispel." In *Handbook of North American Indians*, vol. 12, *Plateau*, edited by D. E. Walker, 283–296. Washington, DC: Smithsonian Institution.

Lang, G. 2008. *Making Wawa: The Genesis of Chinook Jargon*. Vancouver: University of British Columbia Press.

Lewis, D. G., E. Thorsgard, and C. Williams. 2013. "Honoring Our Tilixam: Chinookan People of Grand Ronde." In *Chinookan Peoples of the Lower Columbia*, edited by R. T. Boyd, K. A. Ames, and T. A. Johnson, 307–325. Seattle: University of Washington Press.

Malouf, C. I. 1998. "Flathead and Pend d'Oreille." In *Handbook of North American Indians,* vol. 12, *Plateau,* edited by D. E. Walker Jr., 297–312. Washington, DC: Smithsonian Institution.

McArthur, L. A. 1992. *Oregon Geographic Names.* 6th ed. Portland: Oregon Historical Society Press.

McClosky, D. 2014. Cascadia. Map. Cascadia Institute. Cascadia-Institute.org.

Meany, E. S. 1923. *Origin of Washington Geographic Names.* Seattle: University of Washington Press.

Meany, E. S. 1957. *Vancouver's Discovery of Puget Sound.* Portland, OR: Binford and Mort.

Richardson, A., and B. Galloway. 2011. *Nooksack Place Names: Geography, Culture, and Language.* Vancouver: University of British Columbia Press.

Richardson, A., and T. A. Lloyd. 2014. "Koma Kulshan: The Misnaming of a Mountain." *Journal of the Whatcom County Historical Society* 14:64–85.

Ross, J. A. 1998. "Spokane." In *Handbook of North American Indians,* vol. 12, *Plateau,* edited by D. E. Walker Jr., 271–282. Washington, DC: Smithsonian Institution.

Schuster, H. H. 1998. "Yakima and Neighboring Groups." In *Handbook of North American Indians,* vol. 12, *Plateau,* edited by D. E. Walker Jr., 327–351. Washington, DC: Smithsonian Institution.

Seaburg, W. R., and J. Miller. 1990. "Tillamook." In *Handbook of North American Indians,* vol. 7, *Northwest Coast,* edited by W. Suttles, 560–567. Washington, DC: Smithsonian Institution.

Silverstein, M. 1990. "Chinookans of the Lower Columbia." In *Handbook of North American Indians,* vol. 7, *Northwest Coast,* edited by W. Suttles, 533–546. Washington, DC: Smithsonian Institution.

Sprague, R. 1998. "Palouse." In *Handbook of North American Indians,* vol. 12, *Plateau,* edited by D. E. Walker Jr., 352–359. Washington, DC: Smithsonian Institution.

Stern, T. 1998. "Klamath and Modoc." In *Handbook of North American Indians,* vol. 12, *Plateau,* edited by E. Walker Jr., 446–466. Washington, DC: Smithsonian Institution.

Sund, R. 2004. *Poems from Ish River Country.* Washington, DC: Shoemaker and Hoard.

Suttles, W., and B. Lane. 1990. "Southern Coast Salish." In *Handbook of North American Indians,* vol. 7, *Northwest Coast,* edited by W. Suttles, 485–502. Washington, DC: Smithsonian Institution.

Thomas, E. H. 1970. *Chinook: A History and Dictionary of the Northwest Coast Trade Jargon.* Portland, OR: Binford and Mort.

Thrush, C. 2007. *Native Seattle: Histories from the Crossing-Over Place.* Seattle: University of Washington Press.

Tucker, D. 2015. *Geology Underfoot in Western Washington.* Missoula, MT: Mountain Press.

USGS. 2015. "Old Name Officially Returns to Nation's Highest Peak." *USGS Science Feature*s. https://www2.usgs.gov/blogs/features/usgs_top_story/old-name-restored-to-nations-highest-peak/.

Winthrop, T. 1863. *The Canoe and the Saddle.* Boston, MA: Ticknor and Fields.

PART 2

Indigenous Voices

KRISTIN DENHAM

In chapters 3 through 5, the authors describe ways in which colonization has affected the languages of the Indigenous peoples who have long occupied the Pacific Northwest region. Building on some of the historical background from part 1, these authors examine the current linguistic situations of many of the Indigenous groups of the region.

In chapter 3, "Indigenous Language Revitalization in the Pacific Northwest," Russell Hugo provides an overview of language revitalization programs of various Native American languages that have ceased to be spoken by children and what is being done to preserve, revitalize, and actively engage with these languages. He includes discussions of the partnerships with schools and universities to illustrate the varied ways in which Indigenous communities' languages are not only surviving but are in some cases thriving.

In chapter 4, "Reviving Chinook Jargon: The Chinuk Wawa Language Program of the Confederated Tribes of Grand Ronde, Oregon," Henry Zenk and Kathy Cole offer a thorough exploration of Chinuk Wawa, the language, often described as a pidgin language, that was used throughout the region at the time of contact with Europeans. They describe the ways that this "unifying" language not only allowed for widespread communication across speakers of many languages throughout and beyond this region, but also has continued to change and to serve as a unifying force in the Grand Ronde community. The documents and field notes in the language offer important insight into the role of the language in the nineteenth and twentieth centuries, and the discussion of the current language program at the

Confederated Tribes of Grand Ronde shows how the language continues to thrive in the twenty-first century.

In chapter 5, "Indigenous Language Revitalization on Puyallup Territory," Danica Sterud Miller discusses the very real and continued trauma that results from the damage wrought by Indian boarding schools and the attempts to eliminate language and identity. She offers a personal account of the launching the Lushootseed Language Institute and the importance of embracing an Indigenous model of instruction.

These chapters clearly convey how any discussion of the languages of our region must include a thorough investigation of the Indigenous peoples and how they continue to not only survive but also to thrive in the face of tremendous discrimination and adversity.

3

Indigenous Language Revitalization in the Pacific Northwest

RUSSELL HUGO

The Pacific Northwest (PNW) is home to a great number of Indigenous languages. Although detailed information about the status of all these languages is not available, research does exist on what languages were originally spoken in the region when contact with Europeans first occurred, roughly around the late eighteenth century (Gunther 1972). Figure 3.1 (on next page) shows a portion of the region and the boundaries of where these languages were spoken at that time.[1]

The current status of most Indigenous languages in the United States does not inspire much hope (Lee and McLaughlin 2001; Living Tongues 2016a). Of the original estimated three hundred languages that existed prior to European contact in North America, only about 155 were believed to still be spoken in 1998 (Krauss 1998). Of these 155 languages, more than 70 percent are spoken only by those in the grandparent generation or older, and all Indigenous languages in the continental United States are severely endangered.[2] Krauss predicted that, by 2060, only twenty languages will still have people who speak them as a first (L1), or dominantly fluent, language.[3] Certain areas of North America face higher levels of extinction. Hinton (1998) notes that of the ninety-eight languages that were once spoken in California, almost none had any L1 speakers remaining at the time of her publication. Even the languages that had speakers were not being used in daily communication. This form and rate of extinction does not have historical precedent and is similar to cultural diversity loss (Crawford 2000; FPHLCC 2010; Hale et al. 1992; Sachdev 1995).

There are more Indigenous languages in the Pacific Northwest than in many other parts of North America, especially when compared to other more heavily populated areas of the East Coast. This is likely partly due to

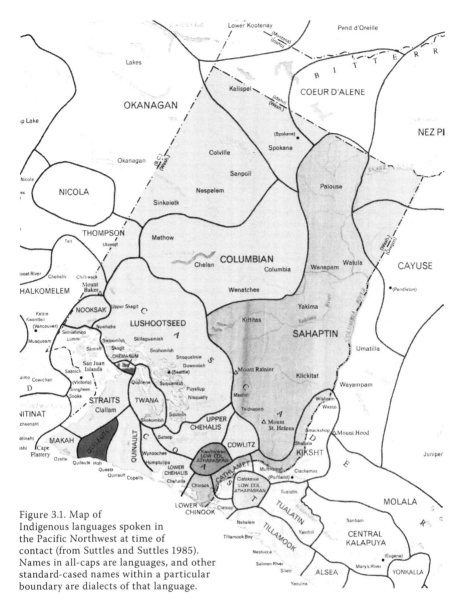

Figure 3.1. Map of Indigenous languages spoken in the Pacific Northwest at time of contact (from Suttles and Suttles 1985). Names in all-caps are languages, and other standard-cased names within a particular boundary are dialects of that language.

populations having later contact with non-Indigenous people. However, all PNW languages are facing extinction in the coming decades. The Living Tongues Institute for Endangered Languages identifies the Pacific Northwest region as one of the five most threatened hotspots in the world (Living Tongues 2016b). Their labeling accounts for not only the number of living speakers but also how much of the language is left to be recorded and preserved, a process referred to as "language documentation" by linguists. If a language is not heavily documented and few speakers remain, it becomes incredibly difficult, if not seemingly impossible in some cases, to revitalize it. Linguists throughout the PNW are working hard to document what they can for future generations while elder speakers are still alive.

Thirty-four Indigenous languages fall within the borders of British Columbia, and current estimates put the fluent speaker population for all languages combined at 5,289 people, or roughly 4 percent of the Indigenous population (FPCC 2014). In Washington State, of the twenty-four languages spoken at the time of contact, only six were reported as being taught in at least one K–12 school in 2009 (Hugo 2010). The population of speakers of Indigenous languages spoken within the borders of Oregon and Idaho is also rapidly declining (Lewis, Simons, and Fennig 2013).

WHY DO INDIGENOUS LANGUAGES MATTER?

A study by Hugo (2015) found that some non-Indigenous people (who reside in the PNW near Indigenous reservations) devalue Indigenous languages because of the perceived limited economic advantages the languages provide and a perceived lack of modern utility.[4] In North America, some individuals believe that there is little value in being competent in multiple languages, regardless of whether they are Indigenous. Some argue that minority languages should be abandoned so that their speakers can assimilate and succeed socially (Hale et al. 1992; House 2002). Indigenous languages may be seen as destined to die in a way that follows one particular interpretation of the concept of "survival of the fittest" (Crawford 2000). Opinions of this nature do exist in popular thought (Lee and McLaughlin 2001), although to what extent is unknown. The following quote illustrates one particular view on the inevitability of language death in relation to the global dominance of English and other major languages.

> At the end of the day, language death is, ironically, a symptom of people coming together. Globalization means hitherto isolated peoples migrating and sharing space. . . . The alternative, it would seem, is Indigenous groups left to live in isolation—complete with the maltreatment of women and lack of access to modern medicine and technology typical of such societies. Few could countenance this as morally justified, and attempts to find some happy medium in such cases are frustrated by the simple fact that such peoples, upon exposure to the West, tend to seek membership in it. (McWhorter 2009, 16)

McWhorter suggests that globalism is a root cause of language death and takes an arguably pragmatic view. He asks the reader to ponder the value of linguistic diversity compared with linguistic unity. Yet, in that excerpt, minority languages are also tangentially associated (via the term "Indigenous groups") with the oppression of women and ignorance, or at least militant or negligent isolationism. These assertions are all highly questionable and offensive, especially without data to back them up. Another controversial statement is that the people exposed to the "West" will generally desire to be assimilated into the culture. This is an especially problematic view seen through the historical and present context of the PNW of North America, as well as many other places where colonialism, forced migration, and forced assimilation have left their devastating effects. McWhorter also argues that the core loss associated with language death is primarily aesthetic and not cultural: "Native American groups would bristle at the idea that they are no longer meaningfully 'Indian' simply because they no longer speak their ancestral tongue" (2009, 15). However, this assumption is simply not observable in most, if not all, Indigenous communities. Indigenous scholars, activists and citizens often state the important role language plays in culture and identity. The quotes above are examples of the types of opinions held by non-Indigenous individuals. They also illustrate the ongoing process of colonialism as well as the idea that monolingualism is rooted largely in ideology and politics. But the goal of most, if not all, revitalization efforts is not to replace English, but instead to develop a bilingual and bicultural environment for future generations. It is highly unlikely that in the foreseeable future any of the citizens of North American Indigenous Nations will abandon English, given its dominant economic status and cultural presence (Tse 2001). Instead, a balance must be found between the dominant external culture and the local minority community's culture, and language is a key part of that cultural balance (Grimes 1998).

Why then, should anyone concern themselves with trying to improve the vitality of languages that are seemingly fated for extinction? Crawford (2000) presents the following argument:

Along with the accompanying loss of culture, language loss can destroy a sense of self-worth, limiting human potential and complicating efforts to solve other problems, such as poverty, family break down, school failure, and substance abuse. After all,

> language death does not happen in privileged communities. It
> happens to the dispossessed and the disempowered, peoples who
> most need their cultural resources to survive. (Crawford 2000, 63)[5]

The issues that Crawford describes are highly interconnected. Without sufficient financial and other practical resources, the cultural foundations and political stability of a group can be further threatened.[6] For example, in the United States, language can play a role in determining federal recognition of an Indigenous group as an independent nation (Administrative Committee of the Federal Registrar 2001). Language can be encoded with, and linked to, culture. When a language disappears, the entire world loses precious scientific, anthropological, historical, and linguistic information. In addition to some of these more objective arguments supporting revitalization and preservation efforts, the social justice perspective should also be considered. North American Indigenous languages were eradicated by government policy (Adams 1995; McCarty 1998; Reyhner 1992, 1993), and their decline is a by-product of many atrocities stemming from colonization. Describing the loss of these languages as a natural or inevitable process is not accurate. Throughout North America, an entire generation of Indigenous children were forcibly removed from their homes and communities and made to live in boarding schools, where they were punished for speaking their languages. As Jacob (2013), a citizen of the Yakama Nation, argues, colonialism is not a past event, it is an ongoing process. Language revitalization is a crucial part of the process of decolonization. In some instances, it is vital to political power, especially as it relates to sovereignty.

POLICY

Around the 1960s, many external (i.e., colonialist state, provincial, and federal) governments slowly began changing policies from trying to eradicate Indigenous languages to permitting, and even sometimes encouraging, Indigenous nations to teach, learn and speak them again. Although some governments have now publicly begun to acknowledge the crimes and some have attempted to account for them in various ways, the effort has for the most part been far too little and much too late. Even some of the largest efforts to provide funding for language programs have been failures. Financial support from the US federal government for Indigenous language education was intermittent in the more recent past (i.e., 1960–1980s)

(Spolsky 1977), although funding did become more accessible throughout the 1990s (Hinton 1998). This lack of stability forced programs to cease or drastically reduce their scope, which in turn led to resentment and a lack of trust of the state and federal government to follow through on such programs (Fishman 2001).

Since 1990, some more positive changes have come from US and Canadian governments. In the United States, 1990 saw the passage of the Native American Languages Act (101st Congress 1990) which has generally been seen as beneficial. At the state level, the Washington State Senate passed Senate Bill 5269 (2007), which loosened the restrictions on language-teacher certification for "first peoples." In 2003, the Washington State Board of Education enacted WAC 181-78A-700, which created a system of certification intended to be a localized partnership between each individual tribe and the state. SB5269 also contains language that encourages higher-education institutions to grant Native American languages equal credit value as "foreign" (or world) languages.[7] Also, additional legislation (HB1495, 2005–2006) mandates the instruction of Indigenous (tribal) history in public schools (Representatives et al. 2005).

Although the changes above are welcomed for the most part, US state governments and their educational oversight institutions are generally much more ignorant of and less attentive to Indigenous language education than are their Canadian counterparts. As one example, the Office of the Superintendent of Public Instruction for the state of Washington has only limited knowledge of which languages are being taught in K–12 schools, and support is lacking (Hugo 2010).[8] Although still far from crafting a perfect situation, the government of British Columbia invests much more than any PNW US state into supporting Indigenous languages. The First People's Cultural Council (FPCC) has no peer in the US PNW when it comes to monitoring and institutional support. The council has to date published two robust reports on the status of Indigenous languages, the latest in 2014 (FPCC 2014), and it supports the development of new resources and research to promote Indigenous language vitality. One of the FPCC's more prominent projects is the First Voices website, which provides a space in which members of every Indigenous language community in Canada can collaborate and present basic learning materials for the language and culture. Some of the tools they provide include the ability to create an online dictionary, media files, online lessons, and applications for typing in the alphabet/orthography of the language.

EDUCATION: UNIVERSITY COLLABORATION

One of the key partnerships in efforts to revitalize languages is that between universities and local Indigenous nations. Below I highlight a few of the most active institutions and recent key projects that they are engaged in.[9]

Canada

Simon Fraser University

Simon Fraser University's (SFU) First Nations Language Centre has been and continues to be a strong advocate and ally for the Indigenous languages of Western Canada. The Centre is headed by Dr. Marianne Ignace, who is the author of many language resources, including the *Handbook of Aboriginal Language Program Planning in British Columbia*. One of the more recent successes of the Centre is a substantial partnership grant that has allowed them to begin a seven-year-long project to collaborate with at least twenty-two "community-based First Nations groups that are dedicated to maintaining and revitalizing indigenous dialects" (First Nations Language Centre 2016b).

Kwi Awt Stelmexw is an institution of the Squamish Nation, located in what is now known as British Columbia, that supports culture and language vitalization. Around 2017, it began a partnership with Simon Fraser University to offer a full-time intensive adult immersion program that runs for at least six months.[10] Students who complete the program will have had at least a thousand hours of contact time with the language (Kwi Awt Stelmexw 2016). Kwi Awt Stelmexw has also been awarded funding from the First Peoples' Cultural Council to undertake a study and develop a twenty-five-year action plan for the language.

University of Victoria

The University of Victoria (UVIC) has an extensive offering of courses related to Indigenous language education, including a Certificate in Aboriginal Language Revitalization (CALR) that "enables individuals concerned with language loss, maintenance, and recovery to develop both knowledge and practical strategies for language revitalization activities across British Columbia and beyond" (University of Victoria 2016).

University of British Columbia

The University of British Columbia's First Nations and Endangered Languages Program (FNEL) offers courses in the Musqueam language, which is the language traditionally spoken on the land where FNEL resides. The majority of the other courses offered by FNEL emphasize documentation skills, which fits very well, in the region, with the somewhat more pedagogically focused missions of UVIC and SFU. If languages are to be revitalized by educators, it is necessary they first be conserved and preserved.

The University of British Columbia Press also recently published a volume of Lushootseed texts (Beck and Hess 2014), which has accompanying detailed grammatical and stylistic analyses. Another aspect that makes this publication such a valuable resource for educators and researchers are the morphological glosses[11] for all of the entries.

United States
Northwest Indian Language Institute

Arguably the most active and robust higher education–based organization that supports Indigenous languages in the PNW of the contiguous United States is the Northwest Indian Language Institute, or NILI (pronounced "nee-lee"). NILI is located at the University of Oregon in Eugene, Oregon, but its work reaches well beyond the borders of the state. For example, NILI has a strong collaborative tie with Yakama/Yakima (or Ichishkíin Sínwit) language educators in the Yakama Nation, which is located in what is now Eastern Washington State. A recently published grammar of the Yakama language by Dr. Joana Jansen of NILI is just one highlight (Jansen 2010). The institute supports teacher training and resource development and offers a highly regarded summer institute for local language activists and educators on basic linguistics, classroom pedagogy, and creating pedagogical materials.

University of Washington

The American Indian Studies Department at the University of Washington (UW) has been working with local instructors to offer informal (i.e., not for credit) Southern Lushootseed classes every two weeks. Currently, the only formal (for credit) Indigenous-language course offered at the university is for Inuktitut (a language originating from Nunavut, not from the PNW), which is taught remotely by an instructor who teleconferences into a classroom. The Canadian Studies Center of the Jackson School of International Studies has been supporting this course offering, and there has been an ongoing collaboration with the university's Language Learning Center to create a fully online course for Inuktitut 101.

Individuals across campus are also at work on a variety of efforts. A long-term collaboration between UW linguistics professor Sharon Hargus and Yakama elder Dr. Virginia Beavert has resulted in the publication of a dictionary for Yakama (Beavert and Hargus 2009). The UW Language Learning Center has been working with the Tulalip Lushootseed Language Program to develop online course content for their classes as well as a fully online mini-course for community members. In addition, the center hosts and maintains online archives of learning materials for Yakama (Ichishkíin Sínwit) and Lushootseed.

In 2017, the UW Language Learning Center partnered with the Quinault Language Program, the Washington Association for Language Teaching, and Avant Assessment to offer for the first time a language exit requirement test for a local Indigenous language. The language exit requirement test has been offered to UW students who speak a world language that is not taught at the university (e.g., Somali, Punjabi, Dutch). If the students earn a score that is equivalent to Intermediate Low on the ACTFL proficiency scale in both speaking and writing, then they receive three or more high school credits for their language knowledge. Those credits satisfy the exit requirement, which otherwise requires students to take at least one year of language study at the university in order to graduate. Thus, even though Quinault and other Indigenous languages are not offered at UW, knowledge of them, in this capacity, has equal value to all other world languages.[12] These small improvements to formal support will hopefully help demonstrate the value and importance of local Indigenous languages.

Clearly, Indigenous languages have much more extensive formal support in higher education institutions in Western Canada than in the Northwest of the United States. This is likely due in part to more governmental support in Canada, with organizations like the First Peoples' Cultural Council (FPCC) of British Columbia. It may also be related to the greater number of languages with fluent speakers in Canada and better relationships among academic institutions and Indigenous communities.

EDUCATION: K–12 AND COMMUNITY EDUCATION

While universities play an important role in revitalizing Indigenous languages, educational programs in the communities and public schools are even more vital. Unfortunately, nearly all K–12 programs are severely under-resourced and face many struggles. Yet what has been achieved, despite the adversity, is inspiring. Here I present a handful of programs and efforts that provide a snapshot of language education in these contexts. No two language programs are identical, and the resources, politics, history, and culture of each Indigenous nation can have a profound effect on the goals, obstacles, and future of a program.

Makah

The Makah language is spoken in the northwest corner of the Olympic Peninsula of Washington State. It is the only member of the Wakashan language family in the United States, as most of its relatives are spoken on Vancouver Island and in coastal British Columbia. I communicated with Maria Pascua and Janine Ledford, who have been working to revitalize the Makah language for many years, regarding their language program. The Makah Language Program, which was started in 1978, has had many successes but continues to face challenges that are not uncommon with other Indigenous-language programs in the PNW. The program generally consists of five teachers of varying fluency and competence in the language. Teacher turnover is a real concern, as it is difficult and time-consuming to replace and train new individuals.

The youngest students in this program are in the local Head Start classes. Fifteen-minute segments are taught on a regular basis, focusing on language skills and vocabulary young kids might be particularly interested in, such as language relating to food and animals. From kindergarten to eighth grade, a classroom is provided in the local school where students can take fifty-minute Makah classes twice a week. Maria was pleased to report that the 2015–2016 school year was the first time Makah was taught in eighth grade.[13] The program has been teaching Makah at the high school level since 1993, motivated by the passage of the Native American Language Act of 1990 (101st Congress 1990). Around 2016, it began offering a third-year course that will allow students to satisfy college language entrance requirements with Makah. All the schools where the language is taught are public. Janine reports that the collaboration with the public institutions is good, and it seems to have "resulted in improved academic performance." The program continues to offer informal courses for adults, primarily providing a space to learn and practice basic conversational skills. Non-Makah citizens are welcome to take any of the language courses. In fact, Maria believes that having non-Makah learn the language will not only help raise the overall level of the language, but also help promote an understanding of their coastal Indigenous culture and history.

One of the biggest challenges is that about half of Makah citizens reside off the reservation. Maria believes that online courses and video conferencing will be valuable tools for expanding access to the individuals who live too far away to take a traditional class. Although the situation is clearly not without difficulties, the program has seen more children and adults become literate in the language each year. When asked what the goals are for the next five years, Maria said that they hope to create an online course for high school students, develop some online courses for the general community, offer Makah at the college level, and finish an ongoing dictionary project. Since my initial conversation with Maria, the language program has made substantial efforts to secure funding for the dictionary project.

Lushootseed

Lushootseed belongs to the Coast Salish language family; it is spoken by many nations along the coast from British Columbia down into Washington State and is the language belonging to the Seattle area. One of the strongest advocates for the language was Vi (*taqʷšəbluʔ*) Hilbert who worked throughout her life to preserve and teach the language. Her granddaughter, Jill (*tsi sqʷux̌ʷaʔɬ*) La Pointe, continues Vi's work by running the organization Lushootseed Research, which hosts an annual conference for the language as a means for scholars, educators, and learners from various nations and institutions to come together, build ties, and share knowledge (La Pointe 2018).

One example of an educational organization from a Lushootseed-speaking nation is the Tulalip Lushootseed Language Program, which consists of fourteen language instructors as well as some support and technical staff. As in the Makah Language Program, the Tulalip teachers vary with respect to their fluency in, and knowledge of, Lushootseed. They teach classes, starting in day care with babies and toddlers (in order to introduce phonetics, phonology and other linguistic elements). In formal class settings, they teach the language from preschool all the way to the college level. However, their efforts focus on the elementary and college level, including teaching at a local Montessori school and courses through Northwest Indian College. One of their most exciting recent efforts has been to create daily video weather reports in which the spoken language is Lushootseed. These reports are broadcast on the local TV station and through online video services. The program also has developed some language learning games for mobile devices and even for the Nintendo DSi. Tulalip is one of a few other local nations that offer summer language camps for children.

Danica Sterud Miller (this volume), describes the Puyallup Nation's Lushootseed language revitalization efforts and, specifically, the recent Lushootseed Language Institutes in 2016 and 2017 (UW Tacoma 2017). She also provides a necessary examination of the historical and present traumas from colonialism that complicate linguistic vitality and education. Laurel Sercombe (forthcoming) is currently working on an upcoming publication that will provide a thorough history of Lushootseed education all over the region.

Chinuk Wawa

Chinuk Wawa (a variant of Chinook Jargon; see Zenk and Cole, this volume) was spoken throughout the PNW and into northern Canada (Thomason 1983). Arguably, the most active educational movement for Chinuk Wawa has been spearheaded by the Confederated Tribes of Grand Ronde, one of the very few nations/confederations west of the Cascades to offer an immersion program for grades K–5 in an Indigenous language. The history of the language and educational revitalization efforts are explored in much greater detail in chapter 4, but one aspect of recent Chinuk Wawa education is particularly relevant to this overview. Lane Community College in Eugene, Oregon, offered Chinuk Wawa classes that were open to high school and college students. In the spring of 2016, the administration moved to cut the program. Activists quickly responded with rallies and online petitions that resulted in the Board of Education voting in favor of reinstating the language classes. This illustrates another challenge facing many Indigenous-language programs. Once a language program is started, it takes considerable effort to maintain a momentum that can compete with more-commonly-taught languages. Without a critical eye, individuals could infer that a program is either not successful or not in demand. Indigenous and other less-commonly-taught languages need time and support to develop resources, students, and teachers that will help the program grow. If institutional administrators wait until they are able to find 100 percent of the teachers needed, all with full accreditation, and 100 percent of the ideal resources, which are all aesthetically and pedagogically "flawless," then classes will never be offered. Patience with imperfections during the growing process is required for nearly all language programs, but even more so for Indigenous-language programs. The opportunities provided by such programs go beyond students' ability to study a language at an institution of higher learning for credit (for example, they can provide political and social legitimacy for Indigenous languages on campus, develop materials and teacher-training programs, and strengthen links with local communities), and withdrawing them should not be an option. As of March 2018, at least forty students had graduated from a university in Oregon with Chinuk Wawa as their focus language, and for three students it satisfied their language requirement for their master of arts degree (Lane Community College 2018).

CONCLUSION

Given the limitations of space, this chapter could highlight only some of the exciting efforts being undertaken around the PNW to support Indigenous languages. Although many imposing and real challenges still face these languages, it is important for us all to learn from the pragmatic optimism of the many language activists, researchers, educators, and learners. That optimism does not obfuscate the real urgency and need for support and resources. There are no short cuts, and learning a language is difficult. Imagine learning a more widely spoken language, such as Russian, in school or at a university, where students have access to multiple, well-developed, and effective textbooks, fluent and trained teachers, and, most importantly, environments in which the language can be used and students can be truly immersed (e.g., in Russia). Languages in the PNW lack most, if not all, of these advantages. Yet, even in the more ideal situation (i.e., the hypothetical Russian class), robust language learning and acquisition is still incredibly challenging and time consuming.

Because of these factors, strong support for Indigenous language and cultural education is vital. If you are not an Indigenous citizen, you can do your part to support decolonization in a variety of ways. You can raise your voice in support of efforts driven by Indigenous communities throughout the region to teach a local language in your public schools. If you live near a class for the community that is open to noncitizens, you can participate and use the language in public where appropriate (e.g., language nests, coffee shops, and so on). Finally, we can all help by respecting the culture of Indigenous nations and promoting the value of their languages in social spheres so that all Indigenous children are encouraged and supported as they learn.

Notes

1 The boundaries of Washington State are shaded in figure 3.1 to provide some additional frame of reference.

2 A 1992 article by Krauss reported that 80 percent of the three hundred North American Indigenous languages were believed to be moribund (i.e., almost extinct) at that time (Hale et al. 1992).

3 The term *native speaker* is gradually being replaced by *fluent speaker*. *Native speaker* is an imprecise term and difficult to apply in all situations, particularly with "Native" or Indigenous languages. Linguists prefer the term L1 to refer to the primary dominant language an individual speaks, but it may not be the first language they learned, or their birth/heritage language. Counting speakers based on their actual fluency and competency with the language helps us get a more accurate picture of the health of a language.

4 For example, some people questioned how people could communicate about computers in an Indigenous language. Although most Indigenous languages do not have the vocabulary to cover all modern terminology, new words are created frequently and the languages themselves, with additional vocabulary, can handle any subject matter that English, or any other dominant world language, is able to.

5 Crawford is framing the term "survive" in a broader social justice context. Although he doesn't clarify, perhaps a reasonable soft interpretation of this could be related to 'quality of life,' while a moderate one might be 'to thrive' and a strong interpretation would be 'contrary to death, whether cultural, political or physical.' The concern about issues like poverty and substance abuse seem to support a stronger interpretation of the term.

6 See Sterud Miller (this volume), for an excellent example of how Indigenous language knowledge can be critical (in this case, for a legal decision regarding shellfish harvesting rights) in ways that could be unforeseen by many.

7 Most colleges and universities in Washington State require that incoming freshman have at least two years of a "foreign" or "world" language.

8 Efforts to report and document course offerings have arguably improved since the 2010 report.

9 Please understand that it is not possible with the space allotted to mention all the excellent projects being undertaken at an institution by faculty or students. The goal of this section is to provide a rough sketch of the work being done in these arenas. The long, complicated, controversial, and sometimes tragic history between universities and Indigenous communities, although beyond the scope of this chapter, should also be noted. Although it can be argued that many beneficial things have come from past and recent academic research and documentation efforts, exploitation and information theft are just two of the problems that Indigenous communities have faced. For this reason, it is vital to recognize

the need to respect matters such as local oversight of projects, community access, and proper data security.

10   Immersion is a style of language education in which all, or nearly all, of the language used in the classroom is the target language. In a K–12 setting, an immersion school would teach math and history using Chinuk Wawa and not English. Immersion programs are rare, but they are considered one of the gold standards for most, if not all, language education efforts. They require a considerable amount of human, material, and financial resources to launch and, more importantly, sustain.

11   Morphological glosses are, in one sense, detailed diagrams and descriptions of all of the parts of a word, such as prefixes, suffixes, and so on.

12   Indigenous language study at the high school level can also satisfy the entrance and exit requirement as well.

13   Middle school is often the least likely place many Indigenous languages will be taught, mostly because high school provides advantages for college entrance whereas elementary and kindergarten provide continuity along with the language-learning benefits of youth (Herschensohn 2007). All programs would likely wish to offer a full series of courses from K–12, but this is not always feasible, and middle school programs are often the first to be trimmed or the last to be started.

References

101st Congress. 1990. S.2167—Native American Languages Act. https://www.congress.gov/bill/101st-congress/senate-bill/2167.

Adams, D. W. 1995. *Education for Extinction: American Indians and the Boarding School Experience, 1875–1928.* Lawrence: University Press of Kansas.

Administrative Committee of the Federal Registrar. 2001. "Mandatory Criteria for Federal Acknowledgment (25 CFR 83.7)." https://www.law.cornell.edu/cfr/text/25/83.7?qt-cfr_tabs=0#qt-cfr_tabs.

Beavert, V., and S. Hargus. 2009. *Ichishkíin sínwit: Yakama/Yakima Sahaptin Dictionary.* Toppenish/Seattle: Heritage University, in association with University of Washington Press.

Beck, D., and T. Hess. 2014. *Tellings from Our Elders: Lushootseed Syeyehub,* vol. 1, *Snohomish Texts as Told by Martha Williams Lamont, Elizabeth Charles Krise, Edward Sam, and Agnes Jules James.* Vancouver: University of British Columbia Press.

Crawford, J. 2000. *At War with Diversity: US Language Policy in an Age of Anxiety.* Buffalo, NY: Multilingual Matters.

First Nations Language Centre. 2016a. "Mission." http://www.sfu.ca/fnlc/mission.html.

First Nations Language Centre. 2016b. "First Nations Languages in the Twenty-First Century." http://www.sfu.ca/fnlc/Partnership.html.

Fishman, J. A. 2001. *Can Threatened Languages Be Saved? Reversing Language Shift, Revisited: A 21st Century Perspective.* Buffalo, NY: Multilingual Matters.

FPCC. 2014. "2014 Report on the Status of B.C. First Nations Languages." Brentwood Bay, BC: First Peoples' Heritage, Language and Culture Council. http://www.fpcc.ca/files/PDF/Language/FPCC-LanguageReport-141016-WEB.pdf.

FPHLCC. 2010. "2010 Report on the Status of B.C. First Nations Languages. Brentwood Bay, BC: First Peoples' Heritage, Language and Culture Council."

Grimes, C. 1998. "Saving Their Native Tongue." *Sequim Gazette*, January 31, A1 and A5.

Gunther, E. 1972. *Indian Life on the Northwest Coast of North America, as Seen by the Early Explorers and Fur Traders during the Last Decades of the Eighteenth Century.* Chicago: University of Chicago Press.

Hale, K., M. Krauss, L. J. Watahomigie, A. Y. Yamamoto, C. Craig, L. M. Jeanne, and N. C. England. 1992. "Endangered Languages." *Language* 68 (1): 1–42.

Hinton, L. 1998. "Language Loss and Revitalization in California: Overview." *International Journal of the Sociology of Language* 132:83–93.

House, D. 2002. *Language Shift among the Navajos: Identity Politics and Cultural Continuity.* Tucson: University of Arizona Press.

Hugo, R. 2010. Indigenous Language Education in Washington State: Facts, Attitudes and Vitality. Master's thesis, University of Washington, Seattle.

Hugo, R. 2015. "Language Attitudes of Non-Indigenous Individuals Residing Near an Indigenous Community in Washington State." *University of Washington Working Papers in Linguistics* 33.

Ignace, Marianne. 1998. *Handbook of Aboriginal Language Program Planning in British Columbia.* Report Prepared for the First Nations Education Steering Committee Aboriginal Language Sub-Committee, North Vancouver, BC. www.fnesc.ca/publications/pdf/language.pdf.

Jacob, M. 2013. *Yakama Rising: Indigenous Cultural Revitalization, Activism, and Healing.* Tucson: University of Arizona Press.

Jansen, J. W. 2010. A Grammar of Yakima Ichishkíin/Sahaptin. PhD diss., ProQuest Dissertations and Theses, No. 3420340.

Krauss, M. 1998. "The Condition of Native North American Languages: The Need for Realistic Assessment and Action." *International Journal of the Sociology of Language* 132 (1): 9–22.

Kwi Awt Stelmexw. 2016. "Adult Immersion Program." https://www.kwiawtstelmexw.com/immersionprogram/.

Lane Community College. 2018. "Chinuk Wawa." https://www.lanecc.edu/llc/language/chinuk-wawa.

La Pointe, J. 2018. Lushootseed Research. http://www.lushootseedresearch. org/.

Lee, T. S., and D. McLaughlin. 2001. "Reversing Navajo Language Shift, Revisited." In *Can Threatened Languages Be Saved? Reversing Language Shift, Revisited: A 21st Century Perspective*, edited by Joshua A. Fishman. Buffalo, NY: Clevedon.

Lewis, M. P., G. F. Simons, and C. D. Fennig, eds. 2013. *Ethnologue: Languages of the World*. 17th ed. Dallas, TX: SIL International. http://www. ethnologue.com.

Living Tongues. 2016a. "Language Hotpots." http://livingtongues.org/ language-hotspots/.

Living Tongues. 2016b. "Living Tongues Institute for Endangered Languages." http://www.livingtongues.org/.

McCarty, T. L. 1998. "Schooling, Resistance, and American Indian Languages." *International Journal of the Sociology of Language* 132 (1): 27–42.

McWhorter, J. 2009. "The Cosmopolitan Tongue: The Universality of English." *World Affairs* 138 (2): 14–16.

Representatives McCoy, Roach, Simpson, Sullivan, McDermott, et al. 2005. HB 1495, 2005–2006. http://apps.leg.wa.gov/billinfo/summary. aspx?bill=1495&year=2005.

Reyhner, J. 1992. "Policies toward American Indian Languages: A Historical Sketch." In *Language Loyalties: A Source Book on the Official English Controversy*, edited by J. Crawford, 41–47. Chicago: University of Chicago Press.

Reyhner, J. 1993. "American Indian Language Policy and School Success." *Journal of Educational Issues of Language Minority Students* 12 (Special Issue 3, Summer): 35–59.

Sachdev, I. 1995. "Language and Identity: Ethnolinguistic Vitality of Aboriginal Peoples in Canada." *London Journal of Canadian Studies* 11:41–59.

Sercombe, L. Forthcoming. A History of Lushootseed Language Instruction. Manuscript in preparation.

Spolsky, B. 1977. "American Indian Bilingual Education." *Linguistics* 198:57–72.

Sterud Miller, D. (this volume). "Indigenous Language Revitalization on Puyallup Territory."

Suttles, C., and W. P. Suttles (cartographer). 1985. *Native Languages of the Northwest Coast*. Portland, OR: Western Imprints.

Thomason, S. 1983. "Chinook Jargon in a Real and Historical Context." *Language* 59 (4): 820–870. https://www.jstor.org/stable/pdf/413374.pdf.

Tse, L. 2001. "Resisting and Reversing Language Shift: Heritage-Language Resilience among U.S. Native Biliterates." *Harvard Educational Review* 71 (4): 676–709.

University of Victoria. 2016. "Continuing Studies: Certificate in Aboriginal Language Revitalization." https://continuingstudies.uvic.ca/culture-museums-and-indigenous-studies/programs/certificate-in-aboriginal-language-revitalization.

UW Tacoma. 2017. Lushootseed Language Institute. https://digitalcommons.tacoma.uw.edu/lushootseed_institute/.

Zenk, H., and K. Cole. (this volume). "Reviving Chinook Jargon: The Chinuk Wawa Language Program of the Confederated Tribes of Grand Ronde, Oregon."

4

Reviving Chinook Jargon
The Chinuk Wawa Language Program of the Confederated Tribes of Grand Ronde, Oregon

HENRY ZENK AND KATHY COLE
Confederated Tribes of Grand Ronde, Oregon

Grand Ronde Reservation, northwest Oregon, was established in 1856 for the remnant populations of linguistically diverse groups indigenous to Western Oregon's Rogue, Umpqua, and Willamette Valleys. Eight different languages were spoken by treaty-signing tribes relocated to Grand Ronde, while yet more languages were spoken by numbers of individuals married into the original treaty tribes. The pidgin lingua franca of the old Pacific Northwest, usually known as Chinook [tʃʰɪ.nók] Jargon (or in local English, as "Chinook" or as "Jargon") was the original common language of the entire Grand Ronde Reservation community; it became a household language there, learned by many children whose parents spoke different original mother tongues. "Creolization" is the usual linguists' term applied to a pidgin language that undergoes transformation into a language of community and family household. The Grand Ronde community has adopted the language's proper autonym, Chinuk Wawa (spelled *chinuk-wawa* in the alphabet and font developed by the tribe's Chinuk Wawa Language Program), for the creolized form of Chinook Jargon that resulted from that transformation.

Besides being the original common language of the entire Grand Ronde community, Chinuk Wawa also happens to have survived down to the present day, in contrast to all of the Grand Ronde community's other original Indigenous languages. It therefore comes as no surprise that, upon having its legal status as a federally recognized Indian tribe restored (1983) and, subsequently, acquiring the wherewithal to support tribal cultural programs (following the establishment of Spirit Mountain Indian Casino,

1995), the Confederated Tribes of Grand Ronde gave priority to saving and reviving its only remaining Indigenous language—Chinuk Wawa.

Here we first consider the deeper history of Chinuk Wawa, taking as our point of departure the perspective of a member of the first generation of Grand Ronde tribal people born on the reservation. Then, we consider a historical case study of Chinuk Wawa in use in a Grand Ronde community household. And finally, we bring the picture up to the present, with a brief history of the contemporary Chinuk Wawa Language Program of the Confederated Tribes of Grand Ronde.

CHINUK WAWA IN THE EARLIER HISTORY OF THE LOWER COLUMBIA

Chinuk Wawa is a hybrid "contact language" that once sustained interethnic and intertribal communication throughout the Pacific Northwest (Grant 1996; Zenk and Johnson 2013). The hybrid heart of the language consists of elements of distorted Nootkan (Nuuchahnulth) from the west coast of Vancouver Island, fused with a reduced and simplified—but by no means distorted—Lower Chinook, the Indigenous language once spoken at the mouth of Columbia River (Zenk and Johnson 2013, 277–282). The language also incorporates words from Lower Chehalis (a Salishan language spoken just to the north of the mouth of Columbia River), English, French, and a smattering of other (mostly local Indigenous) languages. Scholars agree that the language originated on the lower Columbia River. But just when it originated (whether before or after first contact between local Indigenous people and visiting British and Euro-American seafaring traders) and who contributed the most to its early development and dissemination (whether local Indigenous-language speakers, English-speaking seafaring traders, or French-speaking fur-company employees) are still matters of debate. Rather than recapitulate the disagreements of scholars (see Grant 1996, Lang 2008, and Zenk and Johnson 2013 for accounts of these), we offer for consideration here the perspective of a Grand Ronde elder of an earlier generation. His understanding of the language's historical roots and subsequent rise and decline is not only very succinctly expressed; it is also quite compatible with results of historical scholarship.

The elder was John Warren (1860–1944), the last known speaker of Upper Umpqua Athapaskan, one of the tribal languages of the founding reservation community. Like most other Grand Ronde Indians of his generation, Warren spoke local English and Chinuk Wawa in addition to his natal tribal language. Also in common with other Grand Ronde Indians of his generation, as an adult he used mainly English and Chinuk Wawa within his own family circles. His last surviving daughter, Nora (Warren) Kimsey, who passed away in 2011 at the ripe old age of 102, was among the last surviving community members who had grown up hearing Chinuk Wawa used daily as a household language. Field notes of the Smithsonian linguist John P. Harrington, who interviewed Warren at Grand Ronde in 1940 (Harrington 1981, mf 19.0003—19.0287), document Warren's knowledge both of Chinuk Wawa and of Athapaskan, not to mention his knowledge of local English—as evident in many English anecdotes and reminiscences also appearing there.[1]

According to Warren, Chinuk Wawa was spread primarily by French Canadian fur company employees and their "Chinook" Indian wives (note that historically, the name "Chinook" was often used with reference to any and all of the originally Chinookan-speaking peoples indigenous to the lower Columbia River, from its mouth upstream to The Dalles). This understanding was widely shared by Western Oregon Indigenous people and has received scholarly confirmation most recently from the work of George Lang (2008). It appears that Warren attributed the origin of the language also to these French-Chinook mixed families, a view shared by some other local Indigenous people. Note though that this view was by no means universally shared. For example, one of Zenk's elderly Grand Ronde consultants, Wilson Bobb Sr. (1891–1985), was convinced that the tribes of northwestern Oregon, at least, had "always talked Jargon." Warren's view, as recorded by Harrington (spelling and punctuation as in the original), was this:

The Hudson Bay Company hired a lot of people to trap & hunt for them. They had hqs. at [Fort] Vancouver & elsewhere. they put up those trading posts. But it seems like they were French Canadians, because they came from Canada across into Oregon, they crossed the Columbia river, they came down into Oregon, they had Chinook women for wives, they had no white women, they had to take something, you know. . . . That is why they call it French Prairie now—lots of these Frenchmen settled in there. The orig[inal] ones are pretty nearly all gone. The children survive, these want to come in on our treaty right now. (Harrington 1981, mf 19.0285)

French Prairie extends along the east side of the Willamette River, roughly between the cities of Salem on the south and Newberg on the north. Many French Canadian former Hudson's Bay Company employees settled there with their local Indian wives. Members of a number of these families found their way to Grand Ronde Reservation after it was established in 1856, with the result that the community's tribal rolls show quite a few French surnames. The legal status of at least some members of these families must be what Warren had in mind when he alluded to certain persons wanting "to come in on our treaty."

The hybrid character of Chinuk Wawa and its significance as a lingua franca during the fur trade era were self-evident to Warren, albeit he seems not to have been aware of the Nootkans and their early contribution to Chinuk Wawa. Warren's following observation to Harrington (1981, mf 19.0286) was given largely in Chinuk Wawa, incompletely translated. We accompany Harrington's phonetic transcript (slightly simplified here) with bracketed additions numbered as follows: (1) Warren's Chinuk Wawa, transliterated using the alphabet and standardized spellings of the tribe's contemporary Chinuk Wawa Language Program; (2) a word-for-word (interlinear) literal translation of 1; and (3) a free translation of 1. The Chinuk Wawa appearing in numbered line 1 may be roughly pronounced by reading the vowels as in Spanish or Italian (except for ə, pronounced "uh") and the consonants as in English (skipping over finer points of pronunciation, indicated by certain diacritics and special symbols).

> they learned to talk French, those Ind[ian] women—because that's what they had, Frenchmans, you know,

	sawáac húyhuy wáwɑ	sétkµm sawhuy wáwɑ t's wh́lhµm	wáwɑ,
1)	[shawash huyhuy-wawa	sitkum shawash chinuk-tilixam	wawa,]
2)	[Indian trade-talk	part Indian Chinook-people	talk]
3)	[*The Indian trade language is part Chinook Indian people's language*]		

	sétkµm	pɑsáyµks wáwɑ,
1)	[*sitkum*	*pʰasayuks-wawa,*]
2)	[part	French-talk]
3)	[*part French language,*]	

	sétkµm	páɑstɑn wáwɑ
1)	[*sitkum*	*bastən-wawa*]
2)	[part	English-talk]
3)	[*part English language,*]	

kánaweĕ kâata lɑlɑ́ŋ.

1) [kʰanawi-qʰata lalang]
2) [all-how tongue]
3) [an all-means tongue (Harrington's translation: 'a mixed language').]

Reading somewhat between these lines, it would appear that Warren would have been in basic agreement with Lang's (2008,100–121) case that the Indigenous wives of the French-speaking fur company employees are to be considered the real founders of Chinuk Wawa (at least, of the Chinuk Wawa appearing in mid-nineteenth-century sources and later, with its many French-derived words alongside Indigenously derived words). A point that Warren makes very well is that one of the features of the language contributing to its success in multilingual settings (such as Grand Ronde Reservation) is that it was much easier to learn than the different mother tongues brought into contact in those settings—including English (bastən-wawa, 'Whiteman lingo' in Harrington's translation, below, is the usual Chinuk Wawa term for the English language), which we can only imagine Indigenous people must have found quite difficult to learn—much as English speakers found local Indigenous languages to be, what with their arrays of unfamiliar sounds and their dauntingly complex grammars. Grand Ronde Language Program spellings and standardized word-forms appear bracketed in italic type below; all other text reproduces Harrington's (1981, mf 19.0284) original.

tcɩnúk wáwɑ,
[chinuk-wawa]
the Chin lang. [i.e., Chinuk Wawa] . . .

máykɑ   kámtɑks   tsɩnúk wáwɑ
[mayka   kəmtəks   chinuk-wawa]
do [singular] you understand the Chinook jargon?

'ɑ̀háa, náykɑkɑmtɑks
[aha   nayka kəmtəks]
yes, I understand.

páastɑn wáwɑ   hɑ̀yàac k'âl,
[bastən-wawa   hayash-q'əl]
the Wh[ite]man lingo is awful hard or difficult.

tsɩnúk wáwɑ   wèe k'âl,
[chinuk-wawa   wik-q'əl]
the Chin[ook] jargon is not hard, or difficult.

Warren (Harrington 1981, 19.0286) appears to have attributed the ultimate demise of Chinuk Wawa to a second wave of out-marriages between Indigenous women and outsiders—here, involving English-speaking white men (*bastən* is the usual Chinuk Wawa term for 'Euro-American'; note: the sound written ɬ below can be roughly approximated as "tl").

'áltaǎ   kanaweě ɬákstaǎ   wawa   páastaniǐ wáwa,
[alta   kʰanawi-ɬaksta   wawa   bastən-wawa]
now everybody speaks Eng[lish]

sawáac   hayáactɪkɪ   páastən máan,
[shawash   hayash -tiki   bastən-man]
the Ind[ian] gets stuck on a Wh[ite] man

páastən   hayáactɪkɪ   sawáac ɬútcmən.
[bastən   hayash -tiki   shawash-ɬuchmən]
a wh[ite]m[an] likes an Ind[ian] woman

tcakahîilʉ   tcɪnʉ́k wáwa   'áltaǎ.
[chaku-hilu   chinuk-wawa   alta]
The Chin[ook] jargon is out of date now (is no more).

CHINUK WAWA IN ONE GRAND RONDE COMMUNITY HOUSEHOLD

One Grand Ronde family household may serve as an illustration, both of the household milieu of Chinuk Wawa during the waning days of the segregated reservation community, and of the circumstances that led to the language's near disappearance during that period. The main reason for Chinuk Wawa's near demise was the community's embrace of English, which was universally adopted by younger members of the reservation community, going back to the very first generation of reservation-born Indians.

The household we consider here included an exceptionally long-lived member of the generation just preceding the first one born on the reservation, Mrs. Jennie (Mackey) Riggs (ca. 1846–1937). Jennie Riggs is perhaps the purest known case of a Grand Ronde creole Chinuk Wawa speaker (see Zenk and Johnson 2013, 287). In 1934 the Riggs household included Jennie Riggs, her son Sam Riggs, her daughter-in-law Clara Riggs, and two of the couple's four children. Visiting the household in that year, anthropologist Joel Berreman commented on Jennie Riggs's repertoire of languages: "She talks English with some difficulty. Claims to speak jargon [Chinuk Wawa] fluently, and to be able to understand Clackamas and Klickitat" (Berreman 1935, 53). This information, combined with all that we know of Jennie Riggs's life story, strongly suggests that Chinuk Wawa was her lifelong dominant language. We know, at least, that it must have been so during her entire life at Grand Ronde, where she arrived already a grown child or teenager at the founding of the reservation in 1855–1856.

Zenk (2017) has recently located a heretofore unidentified source of information on Jennie Riggs, consisting of twenty-five pages of field notes transcribed by Elizabeth Jacobs (ca. 1935a), wife of Melville Jacobs, the anthropologist to whom we owe much of our documentation of Western Oregon Indigenous languages, including Chinuk Wawa. These notes lack any accompanying identification as to date, place, and informant; but various details of content and context point unmistakably to Grand Ronde, ca. mid-1930s, and Jennie Riggs. Jacobs recorded these biographical details regarding her unidentified informant: she was an elderly woman; she had never gone to school; her "old folks" apparently were on the run (from the authorities?) before the establishment of the reservation; she came to Grand Ronde in 1855 (the founding date of the reservation); her mother died, whereupon she was raised at Grand Ronde by a Klickitat uncle; her father was "French" from Oregon City, absent in California mining for gold at the time of removal; she was "bought" at Grand Ronde by an Umpqua "big" man, who by implication was an older man, not a young man; she married him "Indian way"; she was the "last one" so married (by implication, at Grand Ronde). That the notes were taken at Grand Ronde is clearly implied: "married Grande Ronde. Been long while here first." Some other manuscript-internal evidence also points to a Grand Ronde provenance and, furthermore, establishes the plausibility of the approximate date (ca. 1935) assigned by Seaburg (1982, 18).[2]

Jennie Riggs's life was independently sketched for Zenk (1978–1993) by her daughter-in-law, Clara Riggs. Many points of close similarity between Jacobs's foregoing sketch and Clara Riggs's accounts make the case that Jennie Riggs was the subject in both cases.[3] Elizabeth Jacobs's transcripts are also of interest in that they appear to provide a by and large faithful record of Jennie Riggs's English, which, as Berreman noted, she "talks with some difficulty" (other community members who knew Jennie Riggs termed her English "broken").[4] Judging by other examples of her fieldwork, Elizabeth Jacobs was quite proficient at catching stylistic nuances of local

English varieties, so we are justified in residing some confidence in this aspect of her record (Youst and Seaburg 2002, 232–234). Here is the main part of Jacobs's foregoing sketch, as it appears in the original. Note that the mystery informant apparently identifies herself in the closing excerpt.

I never school _ my old folks all time in mts. sometimes they nearly catch put them in jail just for that I don't go to school. married Grande [sic] Ronde _ Been long while here first. Only child. my mother sick, she die my kilickitat [sic] uncle raise me. My father french [sic] from Ore. City. He went Calif. to Gold Mine _ that was time all our men folks come here. My father told my people _ you keep that girl _ don't let people drag her round _ Now I went take care my mother _ . (Chinook grandmother, named Maria.) came Grande Ronde (1855). now I stay my uncle. I grow up here. Then that man buy me. Long ago girls not [speak?] _ girls don't go out— they just stay home. They tell me, now you get that man, he's big man he take care you. You get young man maybe he whale you— not take care you good _ you have to run round all over. Then I married him Ind[ian] way. He pay 20 head horses for me—oh pretty horses all. We know him _ he always round kind of _ he was good man. Two wifes died _ 1 he had _ he parted with that woman _ he always stay white people, work _ have cattle, every thing _ he work. . . .

I don't know other people _ I never go away from home _ always at house. no women folk left by Mrs. [sic] Riggs _ just his men folk left. we never keep anybody but his mother's sister.

As caught by Jacobs, some of Jennie Riggs's English patterns and word orders are congruent with Chinuk Wawa patterns and word orders—as noted for the following examples from one of the notebook's two narrative texts: "Red hot that fire" (placement of predicate adjective before sentence subject); "He got to 1 big barn" (numeral "1" used as an indefinite article); "That was king his house the boy got too [sic]" (pronoun resuming noun subject in a possessive construction); "Pretty soon he break their necks" (adverbial phrase preceding pronoun subject and verb); "he want to make 'em go that oxen" (compound causative verb construction placed before noun object). Chinuk Wawa is also virtually devoid of inflectional morphology, perhaps contributing to the speaker's frequent tendency to drop English inflections, as in this additional example showing word orders about equally attributable to English or Chinuk Wawa: "my father tell me I come help you something—what you want." Such features lend added credence to Berreman's observation that while Jennie Riggs spoke English with "some difficulty," she also claimed to (and in point of fact actually did, according to community members who knew her) speak Jargon (Chinuk Wawa) "fluently."

By Clara Riggs's account, Jennie Riggs habitually used a mélange of English and Chinuk Wawa at home. This is illustrated by several attempts that Clara made to recall a folktale she remembered Jennie Riggs telling the children. As it happens, this was one of two narratives that Jennie Riggs also dictated in English (her English) to Elizabeth Jacobs. Although Clara Riggs and Jennie Riggs both took this to be an Indigenous story, it in fact consists of a series of episodes identifiable with the adventures of the French/French Canadian trickster Petit Jean. That name does not appear in Jacobs's transcript, but was half-remembered by Clara Riggs as "John," "Giant" (!), and (more accurately) Jean [ʒɑ·n]. Here is the opening of that narrative in Jacobs's transcript, along with an episode from the subsequent series constituting it:

> [This Indian boy] / She had 1 boy, that woman. A <u>big</u> boy. He
> continued nursing all the time tho so big. The woman got tired.
> "What's the matter that child want to nurse." "you help your father
> _ you big enough now _ you help your father. You make me tired _
> you lay down _ your foot sticks way over there you so tall _ Still you
> nurse _ nurse _ nurse _ go on & help your father cut wood.["] . . .
>
> Then they give him 1 yoke of oxen to plow. "Let him plow that
> garden place." Oh he want to make 'em go that oxen _ he can't. Pretty
> soon he break their necks _ throw oxen way. Then he take that plow
> _ he push _ push _ he plow all that place that want plowed.

And here are corresponding segments from of one of Clara Riggs's renditions (the pronunciation of the Chinuk Wawa may be approximated as explained for the John Warren examples above, with the addition that x is to be pronounced approximately as "ch" in German *Bach*):

> Well that's what she [Jennie Riggs] used to tell the kids you know
> but she'd tell 'em that in the Indian language. 'n that *qʰənchi hayásh*

yax̣ka kʰupa ya pi ya munk-nurse *yaka mama. qʰənchi yuuułqat ya* lay
down *kʰupa* floor. *alta chaku-tʰil yaka mama ya wawa, "mayka łatu! ikta
łush ałqi mayka mamuk! may łatu!"* ...

Then he went on and he got, *ya nanch uk man* have *ya kʰiyutən
hayáq ya* plow. *alta yax̣ka naaanch ikta alta ya mamuk. alta ya łatu yaka
munk uk* took *kʰiyutən* off *ya* took the plow. *alta yaka munk uk* plow
ya kuri-kuri kuri-kuri kuri-kuri ya plow.

[Translation:] Well that's what she used to tell the kids you know
but she'd tell 'em that in the Indian language. 'N that, so very big
he was on her and he nursed his mother. So very long (was) he (as
he) lay down on the floor. Then his mother gets tired of it, she says
"you go! you go do some kind of good! you go!" ...

Then he went on and he got [unfin.], he sees that man have his
horses he's plowing hard. Then he LOOKS (considers) what he'll
do now. Then he goes he did that [unfin.], he took those horses off,
he took the plow then he works the plow, he runs and runs and
runs all around he plows.

Several features typical of Grand Ronde creole Chinuk Wawa are
illustrated in Clara Riggs's short excerpts above. The following are unique
or nearly unique in comparison to the regional Chinook Jargon of the
Pacific Northwest (cf. Zenk 1988, 119–121): *ya* third-person singular
(alongside regional *yaka*); *may* second-person singular (regional *mayka*);
nanch 'see' (regional *nanich*); *munk* for 'make, do' as well as for the causative auxiliary verb (alongside regional *mamuk*, which in Grand Ronde
Chinuk Wawa is more usually heard, as here, as a full verb—'to make,
do, work'); *łatu* [łá·dʊ] 'go' (regional *łat(u)wa*). Note also the third-person
singular pronoun *yax̣ka*, which preserves the original form (versus the
usual regional reduced form *yaka*) of the Chinookan masculine third-
person singular source pronoun. In Grand Ronde Chinuk Wawa, this
form usually serves to focus special attention on a third-person singular
subject, object, or possessor.[5] Finally, note the reduplicated verb-form
kuri-kuri 'run all around,' from *kuri* 'run' (regional *kuli*). This shows Grand
Ronde Chinuk Wawa *r* in a French-derived word (French source: *courir*),
while also providing an illustration in context of Chinuk Wawa productive reduplication, which Robertson (2004) considers to be a definitive
linguistic indicator of creolization.

Also illustrated is the extensive code-switching to English that is characteristic of the language's waning period. Although Clara Riggs was able to converse in Chinuk Wawa with Jennie Riggs, her active Chinuk Wawa vocabulary was rather limited, and she frequently resorted to English code-switches to express her meaning when speaking the language (Zenk's audio recordings from her document this feature at length). Younger household members may have been able to understand much of "grandma's" Chinuk Wawa (Clara Riggs told Zenk yes, they did), but seldom if ever did they attempt to speak it themselves.

THE CONTEMPORARY CHINUK WAWA LANGUAGE PROGRAM OF THE CONFEDERATED TRIBES OF GRAND RONDE

Jennie Riggs was exceptional, even for the elder generation of 1935, in lacking any formal education whatsoever. Almost every Indian child born at the late-nineteenth-century Grand Ronde Reservation had to attend the on-reservation government boarding school, known on the reservation as the "Sisters' School," for the Catholic sisters staffing and teaching it. Children boarded at the school spent the entire school year there, their contacts with their own families restricted to monthly visits. Much has been written about the destructive effects of the old reservation boarding schools on Indigenous cultures. Children boarded at the schools were required to conform to Euro-American norms and use English (although, elder memory and school reports agree, nothing could prevent Grand Ronde children from continuing to speak Chinuk Wawa when by themselves; see Kenoyer, Zenk, and Schrock 2017, 306–307). One thing the school did succeed in accomplishing at Grand Ronde was to extend the benefits of universal English literacy to the children of the reservation. A case in point is the elder John B. Hudson (1866–1954), born at Grand Ronde to a Santiam (Kalapuyan-speaking) family. As an elder, Hudson dictated texts to Melville Jacobs both in Santiam Kalapuya, of which he was one of the last remaining fluent speakers, and in Chinuk Wawa. He was also literate in English, thanks to the two years of his childhood he spent boarded at the Sisters' School. As an adult, he strongly encouraged his own children to pursue their own educations. A son, Emanuel Hudson, graduated from Oregon Agricultural College (precursor of Oregon State University) in 1935; he subsequently earned a master's in education from the same institution and pursued a career in the federal Indian Education system. Two Hudson daughters, Eula (Hudson) Petite and Ila (Hudson)

Dowd, completed courses in education and returned to Grand Ronde as certified public school teachers.

That literacy in English need not preclude fluency in Chinuk Wawa is well illustrated by the examples of Eula and Ila. It was Eula who organized and taught the contemporary community's very first formal Chinuk Wawa classes, begun at the Grand Ronde grade school in 1978 under auspices of a Title IV program. There can be no doubt regarding Eula's English literacy. But she had also grown up with Chinuk Wawa in her childhood home. After retiring from a long teaching career, she chose to put her time and energy into reviving her community's Indigenous heritage, by offering community classes in Chinuk Wawa.

The following historical sketch of the contemporary Chinuk Wawa Language Program of the Confederated Tribes of Grand Ronde is by Kathy Cole and Henry Zenk—hence, the spelling *chinuk-wawa*, used by Kathy and other program participants.

Eula taught *chinuk-wawa* until she passed on in 1986. After that, no formal classes were taught for a while. However, Ila continued to teach informal classes, which were open to the community. We have some of Eula and Ila's lessons, and they are still being used in the language classes being taught presently.

The tribe's present language program dates to 1997, when Tony A. Johnson, a Chinook tribal member from South Bend, Washington, was hired as tribal language specialist. Tony soon learned that Henry Zenk had documented most of the last surviving elder speakers of *chinuk-wawa* during the early 1980s, in the course of a graduate research project in anthropology (other documentation of these speakers is by Hajda 1977–1980). He got in touch with Henry, beginning a collaboration that continued for the entire fourteen years that Tony managed the program. Together, Tony and Henry developed some curriculum materials and commenced teaching community classes in the summer of 1998. Tony set up a database program, with which Henry proceeded to compile the *chinuk-wawa* dictionary database that became the basis of the tribe's published *chinuk-wawa* dictionary (Chinuk Wawa Dictionary Project 2012).

Two tribal members, Jackie (Mercier) Colton Whisler and Bobby Mercier, were the first students certified to teach the language. An immersion preschool was started in 2001 thanks to a grant from the Administration for Native Americans (ANA). Jackie was a natural teacher and was the most successful in getting the kids to speak in the language. She was the lead teacher in that classroom until she passed in 2007. Currently the teachers in the preschool program (discussed more below) are Jeff Mercier, Halona Butler, and Zoey Holsclaw.

ANA grants also funded the creation of curriculum materials, development of which involved the contributions of a number of academically trained friends of the tribe. The Northwest Indian Languages Institute at the University of Oregon has been a full partner of the tribe in the implementation of its ANA grants. The institute's director, Dr. Janne Underriner, along with some of its staff, notably Judith Fernandes, Jerome Viles, Nicholas Viles, and Jaeci Hall, contributed significantly to the development of curriculum materials and the organization of classes. Jerome, a Siletz tribal member, helped Zenk adapt the *chinuk-wawa* database to create an expanded lexicon geared to classroom use. At the encouragement of Dr. Nariyo Kono, a professor of applied linguistics at Portland State University, three students from the department—Sarah Braun Hamilton, Abigail Pecore, and Jedd Schrock—offered their assistance. Pecore helped Zenk with the transcription and digitization of his *chinuk-wawa* field recordings; Braun Hamilton contributed supporting content and handled formatting and book design for the published *chinuk-wawa* dictionary; and Schrock used his own developing *chinuk-wawa* fluency to add to the available selection of *chinuk-wawa* curriculum materials.

In 2004, the language program was expanded with the addition of a kindergarten immersion program taught by Kathy Cole, a tribal member and certified teacher. Cole's kindergarten students went to the local public school in the neighboring town of Willamina, then spent the other half of the day in Grand Ronde speaking *chinuk-wawa*. Whatever they learned at Willamina in English, they were taught in *chinuk-wawa* in Grand Ronde. This method not only taught them to speak *chinuk-wawa*, but it reinforced the concepts that they learned at Willamina. At one point, the *chinuk-wawa* kindergarten class was taught in Willamina as part of the regular school system, but it was difficult for the language to grow because the students were surrounded by English. Therefore, after two years in the public school, it was moved back to Grand Ronde, where it has been ever since.

In 2012, *chinuk-wawa* immersion was offered at the first-grade level, and a grade has been added each year. The students continue to spend half of their day in Willamina and half of their day in Grand Ronde. The class is taught by Ali Holsclaw, with Santi Atanacio and Jade Colton as assistants. They also teach weekly language lessons to a group of K–5 grade and middle school and high school students, the goal being to maintain these students' language levels.

In the 2011–2012 school year, the *chinuk-wawa* class was offered as a foreign language class at Willamina High School, taught by Kathy Cole. The students are able to receive high school and college credit for two years, which in turn fulfills their language requirements for college. Two years of *chinuk-wawa* is also offered at Lane Community College in Eugene (see Hugo, this volume). Language classes are also offered for community members at Chachalu (Grand Ronde's Museum and Culture Center). The community's goal is to reach as many people as possible, so that *chinuk-wawa* will always be spoken in Grand Ronde.

In 2014, Grand Ronde developed a *chinuk-wawa* language app that is now available on iPhones and Android systems. The app includes twenty-seven categories with everything from traditional to modern terms, with games and quizzes for all levels and feedback for each of these categories. There are five stories and five songs in *chinuk-wawa* and English, and more than fifty historical photos with captions.

CONCLUDING NOTE

The Chinuk Wawa Language Program of the Confederated Tribes of Grand Ronde is unique in comparison to other Northwest tribal language programs, in that the language being revived—Chinuk Wawa or creolized Chinook Jargon—was not the original language of any of the Grand Ronde founding tribes. In this chapter, we have tried to show that the elevation of Chinuk Wawa to "tribal language" status at Grand Ronde has been a natural outgrowth of the unique history and character of the Grand Ronde community. Of all of the original languages spoken at Grand Ronde Reservation during the nineteenth century, only Chinuk Wawa survived long enough to be remembered by present-day descendants of the reservation's founders. Quite a few older members of the community retain memories of Chinuk Wawa in use among their own elders. Considering the language's longevity at Grand Ronde, and the fact that there remains virtually no living memory of the community's original tribal languages, it comes as no surprise that the choice of which language to support has not been a big bone of community contention at Grand Ronde—albeit perceptions of whose Chinuk Wawa is best or "correct" may indeed differ.

The samples of Jennie Riggs's English in our section on Chinuk Wawa in a reservation-era household, illustrating (so we suspect) the struggle of a fluent speaker of creole Chinuk Wawa to communicate in a language she had never really mastered—English—present an ironic counterpoint to the mission of the tribe's contemporary Chinuk Wawa Language Program, which is to reintroduce Chinuk Wawa to a community that has been predominantly English-speaking and English-literate for many generations. But literacy in English need not preclude fluency in Chinuk Wawa, as illustrated by the Hudson family. The example of this Grand Ronde family is especially inspirational, since it shows that attaching a positive value to education and advanced English literacy need not be incompatible with also valuing the living link to ancestral heritage afforded by learning the Indigenous language of one's home community.

Of course, Chinuk Wawa remains an endangered language, along with virtually every other Indigenous language still alive in North America. The struggle to revive it remains, in many respects, an uphill battle. The Confederated Tribes of Grand Ronde have responded to this challenge by working to secure the cooperation of a number of public educational institutions in the State of Oregon, while also exploring the potential benefits of modern digital aids—all in an effort to ensure the survival of Chinuk Wawa for future generations.

Notes

1   This section of Harrington's field notes is obscurely referenced, but its source can only have been John Warren. Notes made by Harrington (1981, mf 30.0038) during a January 1940 stay at the home of Elizabeth and Melville Jacobs in Seattle indicate that Melville Jacobs had earlier recorded some Upper Umpqua Athapaskan from Warren (documentation which, unfortunately, appears to have been lost): "Mel says that for a long number of years John Warren, at Grand Ronde, 80 years old & very deaf, has been the sole Indian who knew Upper Umpqua." Harrington himself visited Warren at Grand Ronde, evidently shortly following this Seattle visit. Various local references in the notes prove that they were indeed made at Grand Ronde. Harrington (1981, mf 19.0038) himself notes that John Warren was the source of his re-elicitations of Frachtenberg's Tlatskanai (Clatskanie Athapaskan) vocabulary, which take up a large swath of this section. Many of the latter re-elicitations are accompanied by linguistic examples in Harrington's hand-marked "UU"—for Upper Umpqua Athapaskan. Harrington's most frequent identifying abbreviations in this section are "Winc" and "Wch." An editor's note to 19.0003 reads, "The meaning of the abbreviation 'Winc' has not been determined." Zenk's surmise is that both abbreviations stand for "Winchester," the name of a

pioneer town located a few miles north of Roseburg, Oregon, known also as the location of the main band of Umpquas before their removal to Grand Ronde Reservation. Coquelle Thompson, a speaker of Upper Coquille Athapaskan, identified Warren's language (and Warren himself) as Winchester Umpqua (or "Winsesti," in Thompson's local English) (E. Jacobs 1935b, 1, 46–47, 96, 173).

2   Melville and Elizabeth Jacobs were married in 1931. Since Elizabeth Jacobs accompanied her husband on Western Oregon field trips between 1933 and 1935 (Seaburg in E. Jacobs 2003, 56), it is likely that the twenty-five pages of notebook 131 in her hand were made at Grand Ronde during that period.

3   Clara Riggs reminisced at length on the subject of her mother-in-law's life history. These reminiscences were all captured on audio tape, and have since been digitized and transcribed. The transcripts contain the following biographical particulars, as rearranged in rough chronological order: Jennie Riggs's mother was "Chinook," her father a "White" "Hudson fur trader" named Billy [məkʰáɪ] (cf. "Anne Jenny Mackey," as her name appears in the Grand Ronde Catholic Church register). She and her mother were picked up while fishing "around Oregon City" and put on a ferry to Dayton, Oregon, some twenty-five miles from Grand Ronde. From Dayton, they had an "awful walk" to Grand Ronde, where the newly removed Indians were housed in little cabins with bunkbeds. Her mother was sick (evidently, already when they were picked up by the authorities). Mother died shortly after arrival at Grand Ronde, and Jennie was taken in by her aunt and uncle, Dick Hall (tribal affiliation not mentioned by Clara, but identified as Klickitat in multiple sources) and wife (elsewhere: Nancy). Being of age to marry (Clara thinks Jennie may have been around sixteen on arrival at Grand Ronde), the Halls looked for an eligible man to whom to "sell" her (have her married off in the traditional manner). Finally, they "sold" her off to Solomon Riggs, an Umpqua tribal leader—who was already an "OLD man."

An error for which Zenk bears full responsibility: in Zenk and Johnson (2013, 287) it is stated that "at the age of 17 [Jennie Riggs] was married to the 60-something chief of the Umpqua (Athapaskan-speaking) tribe." Evidence from the Grand Ronde Indian censuses show this assertion, which in retrospect Zenk sees was motivated by taking some of his elder informants' statements too literally, to be quite an exaggeration. Census records show that Solomon Riggs was Jennie Riggs's senior by about twenty years; yes, he was considerably older than she was, but nothing quite like forty-plus years older!

4   Elizabeth Jacobs also transcribed a few Umpqua Athapaskan vocabulary items from her mystery informant: the numerals 1 through 6 and 10, a few expressions—"come on!," "where you going," "go away"—and several vocabulary items—*fire, water, long Indian money, basket ogress*. Since Jennie Riggs lived married to Solomon Riggs, an Upper Umpqua speaker, for over fifty years, it would hardly be surprising had she some experience

of that language, albeit Chinuk Wawa and "broken English" were the only languages anyone else in the community could remember her actually speaking. The predominantly Upper Umpqua focus of notebook 131 is no doubt what led Seaburg (1982, 18) to his conjectured identification of the mystery informant as a "Mrs. Jerden (?)." Elizabeth Jacobs's voluminous field notes from Coquelle Thompson, one of the principal men of Siletz Reservation, identify "Mrs. Jerden" as a Cow Creek Upper Umpqua with some fluency in the language (E. Jacobs ca. 1935b, 1, 46–47, 95, 173). That assessment is borne out by two pages of Upper Umpqua vocabulary items and phrases recorded by Barnett (ca. 1934) from an informant identified as "Jerden." This "Mrs. Jerden" was probably the woman identified as Clara Chapman Jourdan on the 1933 Siletz Reservation census (listed there as an Umpqua Indian, born 1869) and as Mrs. Clara Jordan on the 1910 US census (Siletz Precinct) (listed there as a forty-six-year-old Rogue River Indian, indicated to have spoken English and to have been able to read and write) (June Olson, personal communication 2016; Nicholas Viles, personal communication 2016). If these sources indeed do identify Barnett's "Jerden," the latter person would clearly have been too young and (probably) too proficient in English to have been Jacobs's mystery informant.

5   As in this additional example from Clara Riggs: *yax̣ka ya nanich kʰupa* looking glass! *yáx̣ka!* 'it was she herself she saw in the mirror! she herself.'

References

Barnett, Homer. ca. 1934. Western Oregon fieldnotes. Homer G. Barnett Collection, Box 2, Books 1 and 2, National Anthropological Archives. Washington, DC: Smithsonian Institution.

Berreman, Joel V. 1935. "Field Notes and Various Documents, Research Concerning Cultural Adjustments of the Grand Ronde Indian Tribes, Obtained During the Summer of 1934." Manuscript. The Confederated Tribes of Grand Ronde Cultural Resources Department archives. Grand Ronde, Oregon.

Chinuk Wawa Dictionary Project. 2012. *Chinuk Wawa kakwa nsayka ulman-tilixam ɬaska munk-kəmtəks nsayka / Chinuk Wawa as Our Elders Teach Us to Speak It.* Confederated Tribes of Grand Ronde. Grand Ronde, Oregon.

Grant, Anthony. 1996. "Chinook Jargon and Its Distribution in the Pacific Northwest and Beyond." In *Atlas of Intercultural Communication in the Pacific, Asia, and the Americas*, edited by Stephen A. Wurm, Peter Mülhäusler, and Darrel T. Tryon, 1185–1208. Berlin: De Gruyter Mouton.

Hajda, Yvonne. 1977–1980. Chinuk Wawa data from members of the Grand Ronde community, Oregon: Tapes and tape transcripts. Originals in possession of author; duplicates in the Confederated Tribes of Grand Ronde Cultural Resources Department archives, Grand Ronde, Oregon.

Harrington, John P. 1981. *The Papers of John Peabody Harrington in the Smithsonian Institution, 1907–1957.* Microfilm Edition, Part 1: Alaska/

Northwest Coast. Washington, DC: National Anthropological Archives, Smithsonian Institution.

Jacobs, Elizabeth D. 2003. *The Nehalem Tillamook: An Ethnography.* Edited by William Seaburg. Corvallis: Oregon State University Press.

Jacobs, Elizabeth D. ca. 1935a. Upper Umpqua fieldnotes, informant unidentified. Field notebook no. 131, University of Washington Libraries, Special Collections, Melville Jacobs Papers, Acc. no. 1693-001. Seattle, Washington.

Jacobs, Elizabeth D. ca. 1935b. Narrative texts and ethnographic data in English from Coquelle Thompson. Field notebook 104, University of Washington Libraries, Special Collections, Melville Jacobs papers, Acc. no. 1693-001. Seattle, Washington.

Jacobs, Melville. 1936. "Texts in Chinook Jargon." *University of Washington Publications in Anthropology* 7 (1):1–27.

Kenoyer, Louis, Henry Zenk, and Jedd Schrock. 2017. *My Life, by Louis Kenoyer: Reminiscences of a Grand Ronde Reservation Childhood.* Corvallis: Oregon State University Press.

Lang, George. 2008. *Making Wawa: The Founding of Chinook Jargon.* Vancouver: University of British Columbia Press.

Robertson, David. 2004. "Meanings of Productive Reduplication in Chinuk Wawa of Grand Ronde, Oregon." Manuscript in possession of author.

Seaburg, William. 1982. *Guide to Pacific Northwest Native American Materials in the Melville Jacobs Collection and in Other Archival Collections in the University of Washington Libraries.* Seattle: University of Washington Libraries.

Youst, Lionel, and William R. Seaburg. 2002. *Coquelle Thompson, Athapaskan Witness: A Cultural Biography.* Norman: University of Oklahoma Press.

Zenk, Henry. 1978–1993. Chinuk Wawa and other data from members of the Grand Ronde community, Oregon. Field-notes, sound files, and phonetic transcripts in Confederated Tribes of Grand Ronde Cultural Resources Department archives and in Henry B. Zenk papers, University of Washington Libraries, Special Collections. Grand Ronde, Oregon, and Seattle, Washington.

Zenk, Henry. 1988. "Chinook Jargon in the Speech Community of Grand Ronde Reservation, Oregon: An Ethnography-of-Speaking Approach to an Historical Case of Creolization in Process." *International Journal of the Sociology of Language* 71.

Zenk, Henry. 2017. *Jennie Mackey Riggs: Riggs Family Ancestress—and the Answer to a Mystery.* Grand Ronde History Series. Edited by Briece Edwards. Grand Ronde: Confederated Tribes of Grand Ronde.

Zenk, Henry, and Tony Johnson. 2013. "Chinuk Wawa and Its Roots in Chinookan." In *Chinookan Peoples of the Lower Columbia River*, edited by Robert T. Boyd, Kenneth M. Ames, Tony A. Johnson, 272–287. Seattle: University of Washington Press.

5

Indigenous Language Revitalization on Puyallup Territory

DANICA STERUD MILLER
Puyallup Tribe of Indians
University of Washington Tacoma

Many of us working within Indigenous-language revitalization are fighting several battles. There are the practical battles: What methods do we use? Who has the language fluency to teach, and who has the teaching skills to facilitate language learning and usage? Perhaps most daunting of all, how do we fund the endeavor? And there are the larger, more insidious battles: How do we teach Indigenous languages while acknowledging the trauma of language loss but without replicating the effects? How can we use contemporary educational methods without the inherent bias often contained within those methods? I certainly do not have all the answers, but my hope is that by sharing my experiences I can contribute to the current dialogues in language revitalization and participate in growing our Indigenous practices. This chapter discusses the development and implementation of an Indigenous-language institute and practical applications of Indigenous methodologies into language teaching and learning.

In the last two years, I have had the unique opportunity to work with the Lushootseed revitalization community. Lushootseed, a member of the Salish language family, is the Indigenous language of several Indigenous Coast Salish communities in present-day Washington State. Northern Lushootseed dialect tribes include Skagit, Swinomish, and Snohomish; southern dialect tribes include Snoqualmie, Duwamish, Muckleshoot, Puyallup, Nisqually, and Suquamish (Miller 1999, 13). The Lushootseed language has been thoroughly documented by speakers and linguists alike. Much like most Indigenous languages of the United States, settler colonization, manifested in disease and boarding schools, drastically reduced the numbers of Lushootseed speakers. Lushootseed is currently classified as a moribund language; that is, no children are learning Lushootseed as a first language. In the last decade or so, Lushootseed-speaking communities (Tulalip, Muckleshoot, Squaxin Island, and Puyallup, to a name a few) have begun language revitalization programs. The revitalization model of language acquisition focuses on language production and not, as traditional language teaching has stressed, rote memorization. To create Lushootseed speakers, we need to create language users, not just language learners. The Puyallup Tribe of Indians, for example, supports a very robust language revitalization program; Lushootseed language teachers regularly instruct tribal members, teachers, and other care providers. Chief Leschi, the local Indian school, integrates Lushootseed into daily school activities, as does Grandview, the tribally supported day-care center. By promoting language production over rote memorization, many Indigenous communities, including Lushootseed-speaking peoples, have seen an increase in usage. For Lushootseed specifically, the increase in users has been small, but an increase, nevertheless.

I have always supported Lushootseed revitalization, as both a member of the Puyallup Tribe and a professor at a non-tribal university located on Puyallup territory, and I have consistently strived to integrate Lushootseed into my courses; however, I have not been an active member of the Lushootseed revitalization community. Despite my lack of experience, the Puyallup Tribal Council requested I develop a proposal to submit to the Puyallup language department on the implementation of a Lushootseed immersion program at my home institution. Operating within the correct protocol of my people, I did not suggest to the Puyallup Tribe that they needed a language institute; instead, the Puyallup Tribal Council requested my academic expertise and resource accessibility. Indigenous communities traditionally operate with elders directing and advising the tribal community. Throughout the settler colonial history of the now United States, non-Indigenous people "helping" Indigenous communities have caused as much trauma as the more overt forms of settler colonialism. Although most people working with Indigenous communities are familiar with the dangers of settler colonial benevolence, the trauma such "help" has wrought cannot be overemphasized. It is imperative, then, for all people who work with Indigenous communities to operate within the correct protocol of each Indigenous community. Thus, it is within proper Puyallup protocol that my elders chose a specific role for me. Despite my lack of Lushootseed fluency, I trusted their confidence, and I immediately proposed a summer intensive Lushootseed institute.

WHY REVITALIZE?

Why is revitalization important, and how does language serve our communities, especially our Indigenous communities? For Richard Littlebear, "Embedded in the language are the lessons that guide our daily lives. We cannot leave behind the essence of our being" (2004, 10). As the Indigenous-language eradication policies of the late nineteenth century and into the middle of the twentieth century make clear, the United States understood that Indigenous languages needed to be eradicated in order for tribal communities to fully dissipate. Indigenous language loss cannot be understood as a natural event: "Languages are not so much replaced as displaced. . . . Language shift thus indexes multilayered power inequities" (McCarty 2013, xx). Initially, the loss of Indigenous languages was largely a convenient consequence of settler colonial genocide and disease. In the latter half of the nineteenth century, with the implementation of large-scale industrial boarding schools for Indigenous children, Indigenous language erasure became a federal education policy (McCarty 2013, 37). Throughout the settler colonial United States, Indigenous children were strategically placed into boarding schools where there would be few speakers of their Indigenous language. At boarding schools, speaking Indigenous languages was expressly forbidden, but if a student slipped or dared, the student was subject to varying degrees of punishment that are unequivocally classifiable as abuse. For Lushootseed-speaking peoples, language loss was a direct result of disease and boarding schools. A common belief among the Lower Coast Salish was that speaking Lushootseed in the home was just cause for the children to be removed by the state and sent away to boarding schools. Even though there was no official federal or state policy regarding speaking Lushootseed in the home, the abuses of the federal and state government against Lushootseed-speaking peoples show that a lack of formal policy would not deter most officials from threatening and enforcing fabricated laws.

For Lushootseed-speaking peoples, language loss and the abusive coercion of language eradication methods is a very recent history. The grandparents of my generation learned Lushootseed as their first language (I am forty-two as of the publication of this volume). My grandmother chose out of fear of losing her children to speak only English to them. My father, who grew up on the Puyallup Reservation, heard very little Lushootseed, only the occasional greeting or curse. My family's experience with Lushootseed language loss is typical. We Lower Coast Salish Lushootseed learners are very familiar with our grandparents' fears and punishments regarding speaking Lushootseed. Today's Lushootseed students, therefore, bring a heavy burden into the Lushootseed classroom. In addition to the very serious and ongoing trauma of Indigenous-language loss, efforts at language revitalization have been plagued by academics (often with suspect or, at the very least, unexamined agendas) documenting and codifying the language. Indigenous languages are also in the hands of community elders, again because of settler colonial trauma either directly or indirectly linked to Indigenous-language usage, but the production and teaching of Indigenous language by elders is a complicated process. Western formal education, especially literacy, is "part of and the same process of deliberate and conscious cultural change that has had transcendent social, cultural and economic repercussions for indigenous societies" (Lopez 2008, 56).

DEVELOPING THE LUSHOOTSEED LANGUAGE INSTITUTE

When developing the Lushootseed Language Institute, I had two goals. The first goal was accessibility. We, as Indigenous educators, need to reclaim our Indigenous language outside of formal, Westernized language environments and return our languages back to our communities. At the time that I proposed the institute, the only Lushootseed immersion course was offered through the Northwest Indigenous Language Institute (NILI), which operates at the University of Oregon in Eugene. NILI, by all means a smart and innovative language school, is located hundreds of miles from the traditional territories of Lushootseed-speaking peoples. Participating in NILI's two-week immersion program is both a financial burden and an accessibility issue for many Lushootseed language learners. My proposal emphasized bringing Lushootseed to the people and not, as the only other available option, bringing the people to Lushootseed. In addition, by making tribal community accessibility the priority for language revitalization, we also make Indigenous education methodologies the priority for language revitalization.

Using an Indigenous educational model outside of a Western education paradigm was my second goal when developing the Lushootseed Language Institute. It is not necessarily the case that Western and Indigenous education are at odds, but the standard of Indigenous language teaching must be an Indigenous one. Language revitalization decolonizes the history of Indigenous-language erasure by welcoming the language back into the community and by facilitating the tribal community epistemologies inherent within Indigenous languages. However, in order to fully address the needs of Indigenous students and to honor Indigenous belief paradigms, the educational methodology must be an Indigenous one. Although there are innumerable Indigenous community-specific ways to define Indigenous education, for the purposes of the Lushootseed Language Institute (LLI), I defined "Indigenous educator" (and methods of Indigenous education) as an informal, but integral, community role as a carrier and teacher of tradition, or "auntie education." For Coast Salish peoples, the role of the auntie is central to Indigenous education. Elder women have the maternal responsibility to guide the younger people of the tribe. This responsibility manifests itself in cultural teachings via storytelling, meals, and both general encouragement and admonishment. They are the tribal epistemological guides. For the LLI, using an auntie educational model means teaching Lushootseed in a conversational, encouraging environment, with the expectation that our students will pass on their language knowledge in similar comfortable environments to the larger community.

Indigenous-language revitalization intends to create language users, not language learners. The two primary pedagogical methods for Indigenous-language revitalization are mentoring and language domains. Mentoring involves a student shadowing a fluent speaker until the student attains fluency. Although this one-on-one teaching method has been very successful at creating speakers, its success at creating users has been less so, which suggests that speakers must not only learn the language, they must also be in an environment that necessitates usage. This is where language domains become essential. Language domains, or "nests," are designated areas or rooms exclusively allocated to the use of a specific language. Language nests facilitate language revitalization because language nests facilitates language usage, not just language learning. To revitalize a language, language must be used, and language nests necessitate usage, and, equally importantly, language nests necessitate *contemporary* usage. Lushootseed usage must be intimately integrated with daily activities for Lushootseed to flourish; thus, language nests are often organized in the bathroom or kitchen, rooms we use every day and often. To emphasize the importance of language domains, the LLI had several Lushootseed speakers discuss both the practical aspects of language nests in the home and how language nests helped facilitate their own language usage. Part of the daily curriculum at the LLI has students practicing implementing language nests in their kitchens by using a child's toy kitchen set. Students use rehearsed and spontaneous dialogues to facilitate Lushootseed production. Most students eventually implemented language nests in their own homes (one student even made the family's favorite recliner a language nest!).

Another aspect of Indigenous education integrated into the LLI is curriculum flexibility. Indigenous education is understood to be a dynamic nonlinear process, and to facilitate that dynamism in the LLI classroom, our lectures are built to respond to students' needs, instead of expecting students to engage with our theoretical expectations. Student learning outcomes should always be the course goal, but implementing flexibility within the syllabus and building a classroom environment that trusts student engagement and uses students input as a guide is equally important. For the Lushootseed Language Institute, flexibility was built into the syllabus. As this was only a two-week course, we used student input and teacher analysis to maneuver that flexibility. Every day I discussed with the class and with the teachers what they needed, what they were learning, and what wasn't working. Some days this was done in the full class setting. Other times feedback was accomplished by e-mail, or in groups, or in casual individual conversation. It is important not only that students know that we are invested in their interest, but also that there are various safe ways for students to discuss their opinions.

THE LUSHOOTSEED LANGUAGE INSTITUTE

The Lushootseed Language Institute is a two-week language-immersion course, meeting Monday through Friday, 9 a.m. to 5 p.m. The institute is structured as progressive language acquisition with Indigenous pedagogical methods built in to the teaching methods and modelled for the students to use in their own practice. The first day of the institute begins with a welcoming ceremony that both thanks the Puyallup Tribe and welcomes students to the institute. Not only is the Welcoming Ceremony proper within Puyallup protocol, it also foregrounds the LLI as primarily an Indigenous practice. The Puyallup Tribe of Indians, whose land the host university resides on and who, to a large extent, fund the institute, are known as "the Welcoming People." The Coast Salish people are proud of their hospitable and friendly community. They welcome outsiders and are proud of their generous tables. We have attempted to instill this generosity into our methodology. We are excited about our language, and we want to share our language with the community. Lushootseed language revitalization manifests parts of our Indigenous epistemologies because the LLI continues the spirit of generosity and pride that has always characterized the Puyallup (and the Coast Salish people more generally).

The institute has two Lushootseed language instructors with five assistant language instructors. I teach the non-Lushootseed language classes at the institute. The teachers are community members, whether by tribal affiliation or educational positions, though generally both. The teachers are responsible for creating, developing, and implementing their own course materials, though all teachers work together to develop topics, offer support, and suggest curriculum. Much like the LLI teachers, LLI students are from several Indigenous and community affiliations. In keeping with the Puyallup tradition of welcome and hospitality, the LLI welcomes all students, though we do prioritize students who, in accordance with our Indigenous teaching methodology, have teaching roles in their communities. Again within the Indigenous teaching framework the LLI constructed, prospective students are encouraged to define teaching and community according to the standards of their own communities.

The Lushootseed Language Institute minds Puyallup protocol in several ways: The institute begins with a prayer, song, and drum. Both Puyallup and university leaders speak and are honored with gifts. All of the students were given gifts of tote bags full of Lushootseed learning tools. Every day of the institute we invite elders and other tribal community members to speak about their relationship and experience with Lushootseed and how they use Lushootseed in their daily lives. Another important aspect we are able to include in our institute is a catered breakfast and lunch. Providing lunch means we are able to also offer our guests a meal, as is proper for Coast Salish protocol, and we are also able to spend the lunch hour watching fun Lushootseed videos, listening to Lushootseed songs, and further building our Lushootseed language community. In addition to gifts and food, the LLI also adheres to Puyallup protocol by allowing the LLI curriculum to be available online. With assistance from the host institution's library, all of the lessons, lesson plans, and student projects are available to students and community members alike. Although the LLI does not use the daily course work online in the classroom (students do not need Internet access or computer literacy to be fully integrated in the curriculum), all the curriculum is available online to support students' needs. Further, in regard to Puyallup protocol, all potential Lushootseed learners are welcome to access the site, even if they are not LLI or university students.

Following the Welcoming Ceremony, the first two days of the institute are taught entirely in Lushootseed. During the initial immersion, Lushootseed basics are covered: numbers, alphabet, greetings, and key vocabulary. After the initial immersion, mornings begin with coffee and lectures in English: Indigenous Language Advocacy, Local Tribal Communities, Lushootseed Literature, Coast Salish Geography, Indigenous Tribal Education, and Indigenous Teaching Methods. Although the morning lectures are in English, they are foregrounded with the premise that indigeneity is a land-based epistemology traumatized by settler colonialism. Indigenous language learning cannot be separated from the settler colonial history that attempted to erase it from Indigenous people. A premise of the institute is the knowledge that Indigenous languages are rooted in ancestral epistemologies, which contain strength, power, and sovereignty, and consequently, the damage wrought by settler colonialism is located in the language, but within language revitalization, healing is found, as well. Indigenous language learning must address the trauma of language loss in order to be fully successful. For many of the students and teachers, tears are common as we face, through learning our beautiful language, the enormity of what was stolen.

Following the morning lecture, the rest of the day focuses on Lushootseed language acquisition through the following classes: Introduction to Linguistics, Songs, Conversation, Reclaiming Domains, and Translation. During the second week, the last class of the day focuses on producing a Lushootseed-language video using cell phones. This fun, innovative workshop has students in small groups producing Lushootseed in a very technologically modern yet accessible context, and the class also teaches students how to incorporate everyday technology into language learning. When we originally conceived of the video production lesson, we thought it would be a fun way to produce language and indeed, the students were both spontaneously producing Lushootseed and thoroughly enjoying themselves. Students' feedback echoed that sentiment; so much so, in fact, that many students requested video production every day from the first day. We implemented this request for the second year, and students enthusiastically began producing Lushootseed and recording their progress. For the first week, students recorded scripted dialogue, but for the second, they were given scenarios and vocabulary that they could integrate themselves.

Indigenous language revitalization is a continual process. The LLI's primary goal is increasing Lushootseed usage; however, other concurrent goals are Indigenous language trauma awareness, history and healing, and Indigenous community-building. We have two morning sessions on the history of Indigenous-language eradication and the contemporary Indigenous efforts to revitalize Indigenous languages. However, it is in the two afternoons of cultural sharing that trauma is acknowledged and healing occurs. On both Fridays of the LLI, we put aside the afternoons for cultural sharing. Students are encouraged to bring in songs, stories, or food from their communities. I initially planned these afternoons as a community-building respite from daily Lushootseed immersion. Instead, I witnessed students discuss their personal and family history of language loss, preservation, and dedication to revitalization. Within their deeply painful histories, these unlikely ceremonies helped us acknowledge, process, and begin healing from Indigenous-language theft. The students' stories remind us of the importance of Indigenous language revitalization and how our Indigenous language reconnects us to our ancestors and gives us the strength to persevere under the unforgiving pressures of settler colonization. Simultaneous with the healing of Indigenous language loss is the commitment to Indigenous community. Our students build an intertribal network as they encourage and support each other in the often-frustrating task of language learning and in the daunting task of language teaching and revitalization. The LLI becomes a space, both literally and figuratively, to discuss, implement, and learn different language revitalization methods.

REVITALIZATION/DECOLONIZATION

In *United States v. Washington*, 384 F. Supp. 312 (W.D. Wash. 1974), aff'd, 520 F.2d 676 (9th Cir. 1975), commonly known as the Boldt Decision, Northwest tribal communities argued that, according to the Stevens Treaties, they had the right to the fish harvest. Much to the astonishment of almost everyone involved, the very conservative Judge Boldt agreed. He referenced the language of the treaties, especially this oft-quoted passage:

> The right of taking fish, at all usual and accustomed grounds and
> stations, is further secured to said Indians in common with all
> citizens for the Territory, and of erecting temporary houses for

the purpose of curing, together with the privilege of hunting, gathering roots and berries, and pasturing their horses on open and unclaimed lands; Provided, however, that they shall not take shellfish from any beds staked or cultivated by citizens. (Treaty of Medicine Creek, December 26, 1854, art. III, 10 Stat. 1132)

Judge Boldt ruled that, according to the treaties, local tribes have the right to 50 percent of the fish harvest. The controversial ruling took several years to implement, especially regarding salmon harvests. Whether or not tribes had the right to shellfish harvests, and in what capacity, however, became another lengthy battle that remained unresolved for another twenty years.

Subsequently, in the court case *United States v. Washington*, 873 F. Supp. 1422 (W.D. Wash. 1994), commonly known as Shellfish I, Washington State argued that local tribes did not have the right to 50 percent of shellfish harvest, and more specifically, Washington State argued, local tribes had no claim to geoduck harvests. Geoducks are very large mollusks that live deep below the water's surface along the Salish Sea.[1] The state claimed that because geoducks live far beneath the water's surface, local Indian tribes prior to settler colonialism had not possessed the technology to harvest them. Thus, the state argued, the statute "usual and accustomed places" did not apply, as it was technologically impossible for geoducks to have been known to Northwest Indigenous peoples. In response, Lushootseed-speaking tribes presented the evidence that geoduck is actually a Lushootseed word, $g^widəq$, and not only was geoduck a traditional staple before colonialism, but also the English appropriation of the Lushootseed name suggests local Indigenous peoples introduced the geoduck to the settlers. The court ruled in the tribes' favor.

While geoduck is a rather nifty example of the importance of language revitalization for tribal sovereignty, this example gestures toward more than just a pivotal moment in a drawn-out court drama. Lushootseed speakers know several words that are untranslatable or can be spoken only during ceremony. Geoduck is obviously neither of these types of words, but these situations suggest that within Lushootseed exists—and certainly speakers of Indigenous languages agree—an inherent sovereignty. Indigenous peoples have traditionally constructed their sovereignty in innumerable ways. Sovereignty "insists on the recognition of inherent rights to the respect for political affiliations that are historical and located and for the unique cultural identities that continue to find meaning in those histories and relations" (Barker 2005, 26). The geoduck example straddles both a Coast Salish traditional expression of sovereignty and a Western construction of sovereignty. Coast Salish peoples have always understood themselves as peoples and clans with hunting and fishing rights based on relationships with specific land and water places. The sophisticated technological knowledge required for geoduck harvesting aligns with this traditional understanding of land and water rights, which is how the Coast Salish historically constructed their sovereignty. But the geoduck at the center of the Shellfish I debate also gestures toward contemporary Western constructions of sovereignty as understood through treaty rights and nationhood. Revitalizing Lushootseed returns the Indigenous knowledge for understanding ourselves as a sovereign people within both traditional and Western constructions.

Developing and facilitating the Lushootseed Language Institute is one of the greatest honors my tribe has bestowed on me. The honor and obligation, however, behooves me to admit freely and openly that I barely speak Lushootseed. I have had plenty of starts and finishes, yet Lushootseed will not stick. Despite my frustrating experience with language learning, I am still able, through my academic and tribal connections, to assist in my Indigenous language revitalization. Lushootseed language revitalization "is not merely or even primarily about language per se—that is, it is not about 'saving' an abstraction called language—but is rather about the self-determination of a people, social justice, and the restoration of personal and communal well-being" (McCarty 2013, xx). Settler colonialism has alienated Indigenous peoples from their communities in innumerable ways, but when working within the epistemologies of our ancestors, we are able to resist settler colonialism and regain what was lost, even as imperfect and as complicated as that resistance might be. Settler colonialism has attempted to take our lands, cultures, and languages in many ways, but as long as we honor our inherent indigeneity, however our community constructs it, we can fight those losses.

Notes

1   The Salish Sea is also called Puget Sound.

References

Barker, Joanne. 2005. "For Whom Sovereignty Matters." In *Sovereignty Matters: Locations of Contestation and Possibility in Indigenous Struggles for Self-Determination*, edited by Joanne Barker. Lincoln: University of Nebraska Press.

Hermes, Mary, Megan Bang, and Marin Ananda. 2012. "Designing Indigenous Language Revitalization." *Harvard Educational Review* 82 (3): 381–402.

Littlebear, Richard. 2004. "One Man, Two Languages: Confessions of a Freedom-Loving Bilingual." *Tribal College Journal* 15 (3): 10–12.

Lomawaima, K. T., and T. L. McCarty. 2006. *"To Remain an Indian": Lessons in Democracy from a Century of Native American Education.* New York: Teachers College Press.

Lopez, Luis Enrique. 2008. "Top-Down and Bottom-Up: Counterpoised Visions of Bilingual Intercultural Education in Latin America." In *Can Schools Save Indigenous Languages? Policy and Practice on Four Continents*, edited by Nancy H. Hornberger. New York: Palgrave MacMillan.

McCarty, Teresa L. 2013. *Language Planning and Policy in Native America: History, Theory, Praxis.* Buffalo, NY: Multilingual Matters.

Miller, Jay. 1999. *Lushootseed Culture and the Shamanic Odyssey: An Anchored Radiance.* Lincoln: University of Nebraska Press.

PART 3

English Voices and Attitudes in the Pacific Northwest

KRISTIN DENHAM

In chapters 6, 7, and 8, the authors discuss the features of the English(es) of the region. These chapters delve into some linguistic detail and technicalities that provide necessary background for understanding the pronunciations of many speakers of English in the region.

In chapter 6, "English in the Evergreen State," Alicia Beckford Wassink tells the linguistic story of English in the region and describes the changes taking place, comparing mid-twentieth-century descriptions to features as they exist today. She then considers how these features might differ along ethnic lines. She focuses on pronunciation, analyzing certain features of the speech of Caucasian Americans, Japanese Americans, Mexican Americans, African Americans, and members of the Yakama Indian Nation.

In chapter 7, "Seattle to Spokane: What Washingtonians Think about English Spoken in Their State," Betsy Evans discusses the *perception* of speakers about the English they and those around them speak. Examining what people think about the language of the region, what linguistic features speakers notice most often, and the attitudes that are held about the users of the language reveals a great deal not only about underlying assumptions or misconceptions, but also about ways in which the language varieties might change in the future because of those attitudes.

In chapter 8, "What Oregon English Can Tell Us about Dialect Diversity in the Pacific Northwest," Kara Becker takes data from both production (pronunciation) and perception from native speakers of English in Oregon to help determine whether there is enough evidence to claim a distinctive Pacific Northwest dialect of English. She cites the need for continued investigation of the diversification of English in the Pacific Northwest, where language use and language attitudes work together to affect language change.Z

6

English in the Evergreen State
Nothin' to See Here, Folks! (or Is There?)

ALICIA BECKFORD WASSINK

Washington State enjoys a perception, held by insiders and outsiders alike, that there is nothing to distinguish it dialectally. A common reaction that my study team hears when introducing our research to members of our local community is, "Really, you're studying us? That's interesting. I think of Washington as just kind-of-regular English." The term *dialect*, for the linguist, signifies something different than it does to many non-linguists. A dialect is a linguistic variety associated with a regional aggregate of individuals characterized by shared linguistic forms and common evaluation of those forms. Dialects are characterized by their pronunciation systems and word- and sentence-formation strategies, as well as their vocabulary. Linguists, in fact, find systematic, distinctive features used by both regional and social groups. For this reason, sociolinguists and dialectologists talk about both regional dialects and social dialects (or *sociolects*). Dialects form because unique histories, including settlement patterns that result in separation from other groups, allow linguistic systems to develop in a context of their own that gives them shape.

Among many folks that we encounter in the community, dialects are thought of negatively: they are nonstandard varieties that represent a departure from so-called standard English (Wolfram and Schilling 2015, 2–3). They are considered to be rife with terms that conflict with "proper" English or with local colloquial forms that shouldn't be used in formal writing. Often, people express a negative feeling toward speakers of certain dialects, perhaps attributing to them laziness (Southerners talk with a "drawl"), aggression (New Yorkers talk "fast"), or being "annoying" (such as California Valley girls' use of "uptalk," which describes the pattern in which statements sound like questions, as in "For sure, I just love going to clothing stores and stuff," from Moon Unit Zappa's famous song). Speakers are measured against a model language, real or imagined, that doesn't have these features. Linguists' focus, therefore, is neutral. It says language varieties have forms that make them different from other varieties; these forms have a history that we may identify in our research. Linguists are interested in understanding what that history is, and how the current local context continues to shape how the variety evolves. If these features are distinctive enough to be noticeable, or to be consistent at a regional level, there is *definitely* something to see here. This chapter starts with a brief consideration of linguistically relevant facts pertaining to the history of English in Washington State, as far as facts can be assembled to draw the outlines of the "linguistic story" of English in the region. I then sketch the important changes taking place, insofar as these can be gleaned from early reports and compared with present-day features, and ask whether these features differ along ethnic lines. Using data gathered from a statewide sample of more than one hundred speakers, we examine the key features of Washington English, looking at several vowel-system changes mentioned in the few early dialectological reports conducted in the 1950s and 1960s.

THE STORY OF ENGLISH IN WASHINGTON STATE

We might date the introduction of English in the state to sometime around November 15, 1805, with the arrival to the Pacific Ocean of Captain Meriwether Lewis (1774–1809) and William Clark (1770–1838). Their detailed survey, documenting the plants, animals, geography, and inhabitants of the region, made it possible for Thomas Jefferson to more than double the size of the United States during his presidency. Forty-six years later, a group of twenty-two European Americans became the first trans-American settlers to permanently establish homesteads in what is now the West Seattle neighborhood of Alki Beach (Meany 1946; Sale 1976; Taylor 2003). The leader of the party was Arthur Denny of Illinois. His group was followed over the next several months by settlers from Ohio and New England. The presence of New Englanders was so salient that the Duwamish people generally referred to European American settlers as "Bostons" (a fact also reported by Wolfram and Schilling 2015; see also Battistella and Pippin, this volume). Some travelers arrived via coastal routes from California and Vancouver, Washington. The best information available, therefore, indicates that the most likely locations of origin for the earliest Caucasian speakers to the region include southern Illinois, Ohio, Iowa, Missouri, Indiana, and Massachusetts (Reed 1952).

During the Klondike gold rush of the early 1890s, Seattle established itself as a supply center for the Alaska and Yukon Territories. New transnational migrants, eager to join in the hunt for gold, came from Illinois, Indiana, Ohio, and Missouri (Lee 1957; Lemieux 2005). Drawn by commerce and work on the Northern Pacific Railway, the Chinese became the earliest Asian community in Seattle. By the 1930s, Seattle's Chinatown and Japantown were the largest in the US West. When, during World War II, Japanese Americans were removed in large numbers to inland internment camps under President Roosevelt's Executive Order 9066, some of the vacated homes became occupied by Filipinos and African Americans arriving in the region. Seattle's Yesler Terrace, founded in 1941, became the nation's first racially integrated public housing development. Thus, whereas the period from roughly 1851 to 1940 was characterized by transnational migration into Seattle, the period from 1950–1970 was more centrally associated with the growth of nonwhite minority groups and diversification of Seattle neighborhoods. Some were initially attracted to manufacturing jobs generated during World War II, as government orders for new aircraft increased and Seattle's Boeing Corporation responded. Some arrived for military duty. After the war ended, a brief period of stagnation in manufacturing occurred. However, shortly thereafter, Boeing rose to again play a central role in the local economy, as the focus of airplane manufacturing shifted to passenger aircraft. The African American and Asian American middle classes grew. Their members moved from working-class neighborhoods in the international district to ethnically diverse neighborhoods elsewhere. Seattle was host to the 1962 World's Fair and grew as a center of the arts and visionary thinking. The protests, poetry, and music of "Beats," "Fringies," and "Grunge" artists figured prominently in the American counterculture movement.

The next major phase in local history dates to the establishment of the Microsoft Corporation in 1975. Seattle, to this day, is known for the vitality of its technology and biotechnology sectors, and for the green-collar jobs that signify the city's unique reputation for environmental consciousness. Historians associate this time with both continued trans-coastal migration and an increase in local self-identification (Sale 1976; Taylor 2003). Local pride is evident in neighborhoods such as Ballard, where many families consider themselves to be "true" Seattle natives, distinct from transplants who came to the region for tech jobs.

THE CONTRIBUTIONS OF NONWHITE ETHNICITIES TO WASHINGTON'S CULTURAL LANDSCAPE

It goes without saying that settlers of many backgrounds have made Washington State what it is today. The Pacific Northwest English research study, funded in part by the National Science Foundation, began in 2006. Its two long-term goals are (1) to provide a detailed study of English in the Pacific Northwest, and (2) to investigate the role of contact between different dialects of American English in shaping the contemporary accent(s). Over the years, my teammates and I have had the unique opportunity to include five groups in our study that have had a long history in the region. Indeed, each one has played an important role in shaping the economy and culture of the state. These groupings were Japanese Americans, Mexican Americans, African Americans, members of the Yakama Indian nation, and Caucasian Americans.

The 1880 census provides the earliest record of arrival in the region of Japanese Americans—it lists one speaker. Washington at that point was a territory, not yet a state. By 1890, one year after statehood, Washington had 360 Japanese residents, and by 1910, Seattle's Japantown was the largest in the western United States (Reiff 1981). Most Japanese immigrants worked on the railway system, or in industries such as lumbering, fishing, and agriculture. The Nikkei, or Japanese immigrants and their descendants, worked for lower pay than their Caucasian American counterparts during a time when labor was in short supply (Miyamoto 1963,145). Many lived in rural areas of the state, but those in the urban areas tended to establish small family-run businesses, including laundries, hotels, restaurants, and grocery stores. Even so, they were frequently on the receiving end of racial hostility. In 1941, most of the Japanese population was forcibly removed to internment camps for the duration of World War II by Executive Order 9066 (Daniels 1997). All of our subjects reported that their parents were affected by this measure. Some of our city-dwelling respondents had families that heretofore had lived in ethnically diverse neighborhoods—internment represented the first time their parents had lived together with other Japanese. After the war, many returned to ethnically mixed communities. High levels of regional mobility and interethnic contact is typical in Japanese American families in Washington, and appears to account for the high levels of assimilation of Japanese Americans into Washington culture.

The Mexican American subsample was drawn mainly from the Yakima Valley, in south central Washington. Gamboa (1981) dates the earliest arrival to the Yakima Valley of Mexicans to 1800. The number of Mexicans in Washington grew in the 1930s and 1940s, with systematic recruitment by the United States government in programs like the Yakima Valley Food for Victory Program, an emergency wartime measure designed to remedy the farm labor shortage in the Yakima Valley using *braceros*—Mexican nationals paid to provide migrant labor. Two of the Mexican American speakers were from Spokane. Close friend networks were very similar for all members of this group: fairly evenly divided between Mexican Americans and Caucasians. One reported three close friends of Yakama descent. While most reported hearing some Spanish in the home growing up, only one had used Spanish and English equally in the home. None of the others considered themselves natively fluent in Spanish. Two reported learning Spanish in school.

An interesting fact regarding African American history in Washington State is that the black population emerged quite early. The first African American settler traveled from Massachusetts to California, from there to Vancouver, BC, and arrived in Seattle in 1858, where he was joined by his family shortly thereafter. Others arrived in Seattle in the late 1800s following similar coastal routes, or overland, with jobs on the railway (e.g., porter positions) (Taylor 2003). Besides settling in Seattle, African Americans settled in several small towns along the rail line construction route, such as the coal-mining town of Roslyn, which had a black population of 22 percent in 1900 and was the first town in Washington to have an African American mayor. The African American middle class in Seattle thrived in the 1960s, as is apparent in the existence of early groups such as the Rhinestone Club, the first debutante society for African Americans in the United States (Blackpast.org).

The final nonwhite subsample includes members of the Yakama nation living in traditional reservation lands, constituting 1.3 million acres in the Yakima Valley between the Cascades and the Columbia River. The population of the Yakama in 2000 was 31,799. The Yakama Nation includes the tribes and bands of the Columbia Plateau, including the Palouse, Klickitat, and Yakama. The Yakama figured centrally in the building of intertribal relations by brokering deals among other tribes. They were responsible for

negotiating the 1855 treaty by then-governor Isaac Stevens to end hostilities between the United States military and fourteen Washington State
tribes, who then became members of the Confederated Tribes and Bands
of the Yakama Nation (Yakama Nation Cultural Center 2015). Their contact with other Native groups is confirmed in the comments we have from
subject interviews. For example, a male speaker in our sample volunteered
the information that he spoke Chinuk Wawa (see the chapter by Zenk and
Cole, this volume, pertaining to the use of Chinuk Wawa in Oregon), a
contact variety used in intertribal enterprises such as seasonal trading and
trapping. They reside on traditional lands in south central Washington and
make up 1.8 percent of the present population of the state. English was the
reported primary language of all Yakama subsample speakers, although
two reported that their parents used Yakama Sahaptin in addition to
English in the home. One male in his twenties teaches Yakama Sahaptin to
heritage learners. A female speaker in her forties reported being raised in
a mixed household (one parent Yakama, the other from another western
US First Nation). However, she reported that she commanded only English
with native fluency.

These three broad historic phases (representing sociocultural shifts
from transnational migration to interethnic mixing to regional identification), and the community change they represent, are reflected in the
sampling procedures used in this project. The PNW is still young enough
to include the second generation of non-First-Nation indigenes (folks not
from the Indian populations of the region). Among the nonwhite groupings, we have represented several generations of Indian indigenes, as well
as generations of the immigrant groups just described. It is rare, in dialect
research, to be able to audio-record speakers born this soon after initial
dialect contact, and two generations of speakers following them. Many
sociolinguists understand three generations to suffice for dialect formation
to occur. This is roughly the age of the PNW English dialect region, and so
it represents a ripe time for investigation. Continued study of this community over time will enable tracking of the linguistic evolution in the PNW.

EARLY REPORTS REGARDING WASHINGTON SPEECH

In order for us to describe changes that have taken place in Washington
speech, we first must describe our knowledge of features present in earlier times. Almost the entirety of what we know of Washington speech
comes from the work of Carroll Reed. His writings from the 1950s and

Table 6.1: Reed's 1961 transcription of the vowels of Washington English (with his accompanying keywords)

[i]	three, grease	[u]	*two, tooth*
[ɪ]	six, crib, ear, beard	[ʊ]	*wood, pull, (poor)*
[e]	*eight, April*	[o]	ago, coat, road, home, know
[ɛ]	*ten, egg, head, Mary, stairs, care, (married)*	[ʌ]	sun, brush
[ɚ]	thirty, sermon, furrow	[ɔ]	forty, morning, corn, horse, (poor)
[æ]	*bag, glass, half, aunt, (married)*	[ɑʊ]	down, out, flower
[a]	father, crop, palm, barn, borrow	[ɔɪ]	joint, boil, oil
[ɑɪ]	five, twice, wire		

Source: Reed (1961)

1960s, including the *Linguistic Atlas of the Pacific Northwest* (1965), stand as the most comprehensive description of Washington speech (1952, 1957, 1961, 1965, 1983). Certainly, there are records documenting the settlement history of Washington State, but these accounts don't necessarily provide the linguist with a record of the speech areas those settlers came from. This information must be carefully pieced together from information about the dialect regions where the settlers were born and raised, information that is seldom the focus of migration histories and, worse, is not always available. Reed's research tells us that most of the settlers to the PNW came from Illinois, Iowa, Indiana, Ohio, and Missouri (referred to today as the Upper Midwest or Inland North), with relatively more minor influences from the state of Massachusetts in New England. Reed (1961) states that "most" native speakers in the Pacific Northwest had very standard general American English vowels. His transcriptions of these vowels appear in table 6.1. The pronunciation symbols used are from the International Phonetic Alphabet, or IPA, a guide to which appears in table 6.2.

If we assume that Reed intended to represent the same level of detail in which sociolinguists are now interested, there are five vowels whose qualities appear to have changed appreciably since Reed's research was conducted (shown as italicized items in table 6.1). We'll see below that Washington speech today looks a fair bit different from both earlier Washington English and the English of the Inland North.

VOWEL CHANGES TAKING PLACE IN CONTEMPORARY
WASHINGTON SPEECH

In the early 2000s, a graduate student at the University of Washington, in the Department of Linguistics, took a trip to Australia with a friend. She reported to me that, early in her vacation (the typical weeklong, spring-break variety), she was eating an inexpensive meal at a place similar to what we in the United States might call a "truck stop." While she was enjoying a bowl of soup and some conversation with her traveling companion, a man approached them and asked rather directly, "Hi, are you folks from Washington State?" My student was taken aback by this, because she, like many in the state, didn't think there was anything about her speech to distinguish it, let alone to locate it within a particular part of the United States. Stories like this one motivated me to look closely at the speech of the state. This, and other anecdotes that I heard early in my appointment to the faculty of our department, led me to begin the Pacific Northwest English research study.

To date, 112 individuals have been recorded, in fieldwork sessions taking place either in their homes or in places in their community. Speakers ranged in age from eighteen to ninety-two at the time of recording. Most interviews are 1.5–3 hours in length: first, respondents conversed freely with a friend or family member, then responded to or read a carefully crafted set of materials that allowed us to pinpoint particular aspects of pronunciation.

The results presented here for the Washington study speakers are more fully described in Wassink (2015). As part of this project, Riebold (2015) compared the vowel systems of a subset of the Washington English sample speakers against those described in the published results of three other research studies of other dialect regions (Clopper, Pisoni, and de Jong 2005; Hagiwara 1997; Assmann and Katz 2000). Figures 6.1 and 6.2 (on page 104) compare Washington English to that of two other high-profile dialects in the United States, for convenience. Figure 6.1 compares contemporary

Table 6.2. Plot symbol legend

i	beet	u	boot, fruit
ɪ	bit	ʊ	put
e	bait	o	boat
ɛ	bet	ɔ	bought, caught
æ	bat	ɑ	bot, father

Washington English to that of the Inland North or Midwest—the dialect region to which Reed compared Washington speech in the 1960s—using a small sample of male speech collected by Clopper et al. (2005), including speakers from Wisconsin, Indiana, and western New York. Figure 6.2 presents data from a sample of Southern US English speakers (using a small sample of male Texans, from Assmann and Katz 2000). The dark gray lines in each graph represent the comparison dialect; the light gray lines, the Washington State data. The plot symbols for each vowel category are from the International Phonetic Alphabet, which allows vowels to be represented using unique symbols (see table 6.2).

In the discussion that follows, we paint the broad strokes of the dialect using the data of the Caucasian sample speakers. We then treat the systems of the nonwhite Washingtonians in the section that follows. We draw out commonalities and differences from Reed's early reports to the comparison dialects and also to data discussed in this volume for Oregon English (Becker, this volume). Interested readers who would like to learn about other dialect areas are directed to Labov, Ash, and Boberg (2006), and to Wolfram and Schilling (2015).

The type of representation used in these figures is a very common type of diagram called a *vowel space polygon* (or *vowel quadrilateral*). A full explanation is well outside the scope of this chapter. However, we will introduce some essential concepts that are necessary for understanding the presentation to come in the following pages. (Interested readers are encouraged to learn more about representations of vowel systems in Peter Ladefoged's book, *Vowels and Consonants* 2005.) The symbols plotted on a vowel space diagram represent the key acoustic properties of individual vowels. Looking at the overall shape of the polygon, therefore, gives us a visual way of comparing the "shapes" of the vowel systems of different dialects. Two properties serve as the most reliable cues. In the early days of the phonetic sciences, before the advent of x-ray and computer technology, phoneticians developed a method for representing vowels by the supposed position of the tongue. Two dimensions were used: the highest point or peak of the tongue, and the front or back location of this peak. These dimensions remain conceptually useful. However, recent technological advancements have clarified that what these phoneticians were in fact representing are better understood to be resonating frequencies of the vocal tract, called *formant frequencies*. Formant frequencies represent the vibrational characteristics of air in different locations inside the vocal tract

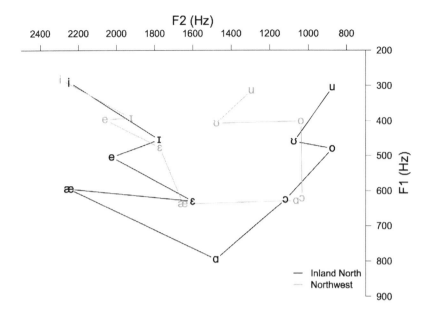

Fig. 6.1. Comparative vowel space polygons. Inland North (Indiana, Wisconsin, western New York) and Washingtonian vowel systems are represented. Light gray: vowel means for the Pacific Northwest study speaker sample. Dark gray line: Inland North speaker sample. Reproduced with permission from John M. Riebold (2015).

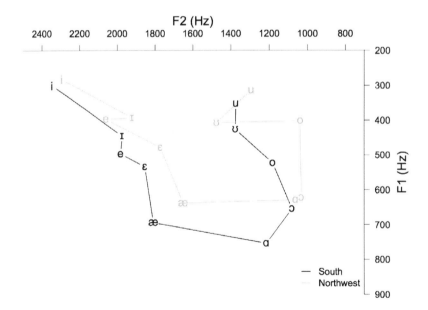

Fig. 6.2. Comparative vowel space polygons. Texan and Washingtonian vowel systems are represented. Light gray: vowel means for the Pacific Northwest study speaker sample. Dark gray line: Southern speaker sample. Reproduced with permission from John M. Riebold (2015).

as the tract takes on complex shapes during vowel production. The first formant frequency, abbreviated F1, has traditionally been associated with the height of the tongue (which shapes the air as it causes narrowing in the vocal tract). The second frequency, abbreviated F2, is taken as a reflection of the combined impacts of lip rounding and the position along the front-to-back axis of the tongue, where the tongue body is highest (which creates bodies of air before and behind the raised tongue). F2 and F1 are plotted as the x and y coordinates, respectively, on a vowel space polygon. The vocal tract takes on particular shapes for particular vowels. We may average standardized values of F1 and F2 over many individual speakers, or for different ages or genders, and plot these averages to obtain an overall depiction of the characteristics of the vowel systems of different groups.

We will take each vowel in turn, moving counterclockwise through the points plotted on the vowel system polygons. Each vowel category is referenced using a keyword (presented below in italics) exemplifying the class, such as BEAT. In the Pacific Northwest English research study, each vowel category was sampled by asking each respondent to produce a common set of words, for inter-speaker comparability, and to balance the effects of different consonants on the formant frequencies of the vowel. For example, the BEAT word class was sampled using a set of "ee" words, including *heed*, *beat*, *bead*, *feel*, *fear*, *teen*, *mean*, *peek*, *creek*, and *eagle*. Each data point in the graph represents the formant frequency averages across all vowels in these words, yielding a vowel category mean for each speaker. The by-speaker vowel category means were then averaged for plotting. In this way, we seek to represent a pronunciation that is closer to the actual average for the speech community. It is furthermore important to note that these graphs do not include all English vowels, just those that are monophthongs. Diphthongal vowels are better represented at multiple time points, and require more complex graphs. We will find it important, from time to time, to make mention of the diphthongal word classes, BOUT, BOY, BITE.

/i/ BEAT. This vowel is very stable across American dialects. Our Washington respondents produce a standard "ee" quality that is very similar to those produced in the Inland North and the US South. We have transcribed this vowel just as Reed did in 1961, which suggests that it has remained unchanged.

/ɪ/ BIT. The vowel in this word class is the first site of between-dialect difference. Washingtonians use a pronunciation that we might consider to be a traditional, general American "ih." Here, Washingtonians differ from Texans, whose pronunciation is diphthongal so that their BIT sounds more akin to "bee-it," and the Midwesterners, whose *milk* can sound more like "melk." This vowel, however, does not appear to have changed in this region since the time of Reed, who transcribed it as we do, [ɪ].

/e/ BAIT. Washingtonians' vowel tends to be longer (duration in milliseconds) and more monophthongal than we find in some US dialects. The quality of this vowel is more like a long, flat "ey." In fact, because of its acoustic characteristics in most North American dialects, this vowel is traditionally considered to be a diphthong. Acoustic measurements do not justify this character-ization for Washington English. The graph shows that the BAIT class is higher along the y-axis than for the comparison dialects. We see this particularly in the speech of young female Caucasian speakers (Freeman 2014; Wassink 2015). Whereas some of the Washington speakers indeed have a general American English "ey" sound, others have a higher vowel, in a pattern that is sufficiently dominant in our speaker sample to raise the sample mean to an F1 similar to that of [ɪ], the "ih" of *bit*. In this way, it is a little different in quality than it was in Reed's day. His records show no evidence of variation in speakers' pronunciation of this vowel. In addition, if the following consonant is "g" (/g/ in the IPA), such as in the word *vague*, we typically see the position of the vowel fall slightly lower along the y-axis, as is discussed in the next paragraph. In terms of our comparison dialects, there are differences to note, as well. For both the Inland North and Southern speakers, /e/ is lower along the y-axis and shifted rightward along the x-axis (further back in the system) than /ɪ/. For Southern speakers, this /e/ vowel is often diphthongal, sounding more like "buh-eyt."

/ɛ/ BET. In one of the most surprising results of our study, we found that the BET class vowels differ significantly depending on the con-sonant following the /ɛ/. If the following consonant is a "g" /g/ or "ng" /ŋ/, the vowel tends to be raised along the y-axis, nearly to the position of, but typically not completely overlapping, the BAIT vowel /e/. So, *beg* tends to sound like "beyg." This is a pattern that we have called "pre-voiced velar raising" ("velar" refers to the location of tongue body contact in the oral cavity when the consonant is articulated, i.e., the velum, or soft palate; "voiced" to the fact that the vocal folds are vibrating for production of the consonant). To the untrained ear (and some trained ones), this vowel indeed sounds like "ey." In one anecdotal account of dialect confusion that has become quite famous in our laboratory, *keg* was confused with *cake* by one student working on the project. As a consequence, he brought the wrong food item (a Boston cream pie) to a college party (instead of beer!). In other consonantal contexts, Washingtonians' /ɛ/ sounds like the standard US English "eh." Thus, *bet*, *head*, and *method* sound much like they do in other standard US English dialects. This yields a sharp division of the /ɛ/ word class into what is effectively two subclasses. Interestingly, this special status was not noted by Reed (who placed *egg* together with *ten* and *head*). Recent research into Californian and Western Canadian varieties of English shows this /ɛ/ vowel, regardless of following consonant, to be positioned more centrally in the vowel polygons, so that *bet* sounds more like *but* (the "uh" vowel class) in both regions. This is of great potential interest to us, because it means that the vowel quality used in Washington English for /ɛ/ is noticeably different from that of the neighboring regions to the north and south of us. In Oregon, there is also evidence of this "ey" pronunciation for /ɛ/, as data in the chapter by Becker (this volume) demonstrates. As far as we can tell from current research, the pre-voiced velar tensing and raising pattern does occur in other US dialects. However, this raising may occur more widely in Washington than in other states. Whereas we find it in other places such as Oregon and Wisconsin (Benson, Fox, and Balkman 2011), it tends to be limited to a few common words, such as *egg*, *beg*, *leg*, and *regular.* Because Washington English is descended from Midwest dialects, we cannot rule out the possibility that we inherited this feature from our eastern ancestors, but if it was present in the earliest varieties of English in the region, it would seem that Reed didn't notice it, or perhaps regarded it as idiosyncratic and chose not to document it. Interestingly, in the western US, this feature appears only in states that border Washington (Montana, Oregon, and possibly Vancouver, British Columbia, but not in Nevada, California, or Arizona; Fridland et al. 2018). In our data, we find it in all eligible words, including words like *length, leggings, peg, measure, treasure,* and *negative.* This pattern differs among speakers. We note, however, that this difference between Washington and other states may be more apparent than real, because this study tested for the phenomenon in a wider range of words than other studies have done to date. More research is under way to test the extent of this pattern for other dialects.

In the US South, the BET vowel takes on an entirely different character, pronounced closer to the diphthongal version of "ey," so that *bet* sounds like "bey-et." And in the Inland North, as figure 6.1 shows, the vowel in BET is often pronounced more like the vowel in BAT /æ/. This makes /ɛ/ one of the most important vowels indicating substantial differences between dialects.

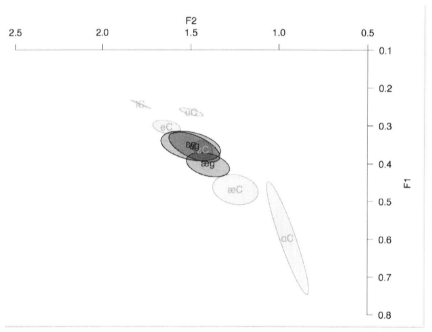

6.3. Vowel space polygon illustrating the common Washington pattern in which BAG /æ/ vowels are raised, and BEG, BAKE /ɛg, eg/ are merged. Data are shown for one female speaker. The "g" beside a vowel indicates the velar subclass; "C" indicates the other consonant environments constituting the other (non-velar) subclass.

/æ/ BAT. In the second part of the pre-voiced velar tensing and raising story begun above with the /ɛ/ BET class, Washington speakers also subdivide the /æ/ word class into two qualities. They produce a raised [æ] in "g" /g/ and "ng" /ŋ/ environments (the voiced velars), so that /æ/ is pronounced very close to "ey," making *bang* sound more like "beyng." This pattern is even more widespread than the raising of /ɛ/ to the vicinity of "ey," described above. As was discussed above, we also find that in BAIT class words, the velar environment is associated with lowering (rather than raising) of the /e/ vowel. The net effect of this is that the /eg, ɛg/ classes are phonetically identical (referred to as "merged" by sociolinguists), with /æg/ raised near to the position of these two vowels. This merger pattern is shown in figure 6.3, which displays the pre-voiced velar environments in dark ellipses, with other landmark vowels describing the outer perimeter of the vowel system in lighter ellipses, for reference ("C" beside a vowel simply indicates the word "consonant," signifying the other, non-velar subclass). When we consider these raising patterns together, we find a combination of features that consistently sets Washington speech apart. *Bag, beg,* and *bake* sound like (near-) homophones to most listeners. Crucially, Reed (1952, 187) specifically noted the raising of [æ] to [eɪ] in words like *hang.* However, he specifically said that it was "infrequent." Note that in table 6.1, *bag* appears as a keyword for the /æ/ class, which is transcribed as a vowel with the same quality that we find in standard US English. The pattern we are describing, therefore, appears to be the extension or progression of a change first noticed by Reed.

We might note, briefly, that although [æ] appears to be in a similar location for both Washingtonians and Southerners in figure 6.2, this plot does not separate the vowel class into the two subclasses mentioned above, masking the difference that recent research has found. Figure 6.1 (Inland North) shows the interesting pattern on which stereotypes of the US Midwest dialect frequently focus: pronunciation of /æ/ so that it sounds like "ey-an," for example, in the woman's name *Ann.* Note that /æ/ for this dialect is much closer to /e/ than it is in the Washington vowel polygon. This pattern is sometimes described as sounding "nasal." In the Inland North, /æ/ is a diphthongal vowel (often transcribed [eæ] or [iæ]) in *all* consonantal environments. In Washington (and other velar raising dialects), it is either [e] or [eɪ], and only in /g/ or /ŋ/ environments.

/ɑ/ BOT, /ɔ/ BOUGHT. In their monumental publication, *The Atlas of North American English*, Labov, Ash, and Boberg (2006) indicate that loss of contrast between the vowels in classes BOT and BOUGHT is one of the defining features of Western American speech. Our research confirms that the qualities of the two vowels are the same for most Washington speakers. This is another case of *merger,* like the /eg, ɛg/ *bake~beg* pattern described above. Speakers of all ages in our Washington study participate in this pattern, with some small differences in the position of the merged vowel. Older speakers' vowels are more distinct acoustically, whereas younger speakers' vowels are more merged, a pattern that suggests the merger is progressing to near-completion over time. This was noticed by Reed (1952, 1961), who noted that "the pronunciation of vowel sounds in words such as *caught* . . . is not differentiated from those in such words as *cot* . . . in the speech of many people" (1952, 186). Mills (1980) confirmed that native listeners cannot differentiate these vowels in listening tests. So, this is not a new feature in Washington speech, nor does it appear to have extended to new words. It may be that it has progressed further toward completion. Washingtonians who retain this vowel appear to do so only in words wherein the consonant that follows is /ɹ/, such as *hoarse* and *mourning.*

It may be seen in figure 6.1 that the Inland North speakers' vowels are spaced quite far apart, with /ɑ/ appearing quite a bit more forward along the x-axis. This is one of the features that makes *father* sound more like "fae-ther" in the Midwest. This loss of contrast means that westerners have one fewer vowel in their system than other US dialects. That indeed seems to be a significant difference between dialect regions.

/o/ BOAT. Washington speakers show a fairly monophthongal /o/. /o/, often represented as [ow], is another vowel that is traditionally understood to be a diphthong in American English. This makes for another difference from the US standard. Also different is its general position in the vowel space polygon. It is in a fairly traditional position, whereas the /o/ produced by the Southern speakers, shown in figure 6.2, is shifted to the left. In fact, other Western dialects (most notably, California and possibly Oregon) use an /o/ vowel that is shifted leftward like the Southern speakers' vowel, so that *boat* sounds more like "beh-owt." Washington speech, therefore, does not share this more general Western feature. Reed (1961) also transcribes this vowel using a monophthongal symbol, indicating that it has remained stable over time.

/ʊ/ PUT. Washington speakers show some leftward shifting of this vowel along the x-axis so that it sounds somewhere between the vowels in *putt* and *pet* (i.e., the mean for this vowel is shifted farther to the left in its position than that of either the Southern or Inland North speakers, although the Southern speakers do show fronting). This is a pattern that was first described for California (Eckert 2005), but has since been described as appearing quite broadly among the Western states (Labov et al. 2006). This vowel class may contain forms from the class we turn to next, /u/. It is not uncommon for some speakers to vary in their production of words like *roof* and *soot*, pronouncing these so that they both rhyme with *put*. This was also a feature of Washington speech in the 1960s (Reed 1961).

/u/ BOOT. Our youngest Washington speakers show extreme fronting of this vowel along the x-axis (positioning to the left of the Inland North speakers' [u]). The resulting pronunciation makes *food* sound more like *feud*. Older speakers tend to either show some fronting, or a more traditional American English "oo" for this vowel. As we can see from figure 6.1, the Inland North does not share this fronting pattern; however, fronting is shared by the Southern speakers. Older speakers vary with regard to this pattern.

Having drawn the general picture of Washington speech (from the perspective of the vowel system of Caucasian speakers), we ask, Do Washington speakers of other backgrounds show similar patterns with regard to participating in these changes?

THE VOWEL SYSTEMS OF WASHINGTON STATE
NONWHITE SPEAKERS

When we turn to the nonwhite speaker groups who were part of this project, the first thing that stands out is that members of the Japanese American sample show overwhelming similarity to the Caucasian speakers. In every respect, the vowel system they show is identical to that of their Anglo counterparts (for vowel graphs, see Wassink 2017). /ɑ/ BOT is completely merged with /ɔ/ BOUGHT. In addition, /u/ is fronted. The pre-voiced velar tensing and raising vowels show some variation between speakers. Because of the history of extensive assimilation of the Japanese Americans into Pacific Northwest culture, described in the historical summary above, we believe this participation in Pacific Northwest vowel changes is easily explained. The social networks of these speakers, more than those of other minority groups in the region, have been more regionally diffuse (and less ethnically insular) since World War II. Japanese Americans and Anglo-Americans sound equally "Washingtonian."

After the Japanese American participants in the study, African American speakers rank next in their participation in the Pacific Northwest vowel system changes, with the exception of the merger of /ɑ/ BOT and /ɔ/ BOUGHT. For this group, these two vowels remain more separate than for our other groups. Considering the pre-voiced velar changes, most of the African Americans we sampled, regardless of age, participate in the raising of *bag* /æ/, confirming its import as a regional dialect feature. Although some speakers in this group merge /eg, ɛg/ *bake, beg*, the overwhelming tendency is to retain a traditional US English position for /ɛg/, avoiding raising or merger with /e/ *bake*. Finally, as was found for the Caucasian and Japanese American speakers, /u/ BOOT is produced in a very fronted position, indicating that African Americans also participate in this feature of Western speech.

Many of the Mexican Americans recorded for this study also show participation in the pre-voiced velar changes: some show raising of /æ/ *bag* as well as merger of /eg, ɛg/ *bake, beg*. The principal difference is in the extent of raising (i.e., not all speakers merged /eg, ɛg/) and gender bias—female speakers' vowels tend to be positioned in closer proximity along the y-axis than male speakers' vowels, suggesting that females are more advanced than male speakers in participation in the change within this ethnic group. (This is not an uncommon finding in sociolinguistic studies of vowel changes, many of which have been similarly "female-led"; see Wolfram and

Schilling 2015, 189, for one discussion.) All Mexican American speakers sampled show merger of /ɑ/ BOT and /ɔ/ BOUGHT. On the other hand, we did not find fronting of /u/ BOOT.

Finally, a look at the Yakama speaker data shows some participation in the Pacific Northwest changes, as well, but less than any other group. There is a robust tendency for /ɑ/ *bot* to be completely merged with /ɔ/ BOUGHT. However, /u/ does not show fronting. Additionally, although the other groups showed participation in the pre-voiced velar tensing and raising vowel changes, the Yakama appear not to. Although their vowel system looks very much like that of the Japanese-, Caucasian-, and Mexican American subsamples in other respects, Yakama speakers are not as advanced in the raising of /æ/ *bag*. Although some speakers do raise /æ/ to some degree, they tend not to raise it as high along the y-axis as the other groups do—both males and females in this group tend to have a more traditional quality for this vowel.

In summary, each of the nonwhite ethnic groups sampled exhibits some pre-voiced velar tensing and raising of /æ/ *bag*. They differ more with regard to the other Pacific Northwest changes, including merger of /eg, ɛg/ *bake* and *beg*, merger of /ɑ/ BOT and /ɔ/ BOUGHT, and fronting of /u/ BOOT. From the descriptive data, Japanese- and Caucasian Americans appear to be somewhat more raised overall. It is very clear that these speakers all "sound Washingtonian," and it is highly likely these form part of a rich set of linguistic resources they command. That is, there are other features particular to some of these groups (African Americans and Yakama in particular) that we may consider "ethnolectal" features. But the Pacific Northwest features appear able to combine with these, so that their speech has both an ethnic and a regional flavor. This topic is taken up further in Wassink (2017).

A PLACE OF OUR OWN IN THE DIALECT LANDSCAPE

We have shown in this chapter that Washingtonians' speech is not "special" in the second of the senses of "dialect" mentioned at the outset of the chapter: it is not regarded as "nonstandard." But it is unlike its neighbors to the North (in Canada) and the South (in California). As will be seen in chapter 8 (by Becker), there are ways in which Oregon resembles Washington, but also resembles California. This emerging picture of differentiation and similarity among coastal Western varieties is one of the reasons that we find Washington English to be of great research interest.

The resulting picture is that Washington speech is not monolithic (it definitely shows some accent variation along ethnic group lines); is not just like the speech of other places where English is also regarded to sound "regular" (such as Ohio and Colorado); and is not just like it was fifty years ago. What we see is that Washington English appears to be a quintessentially standard US dialect (in that it is regarded as "standard English"), while also appearing quintessentially Western. However, this variety of English is, nonetheless, a little bit different from other dialects, in ways significant enough to attract notice, without being stigmatized (see chapter 7, by Evans, which further develops the notion of "ideology of non-accent"). Yes, Washington speakers do have an accent. Washington English has broken away from the Midwestern dialects that provided its earliest forms and continued to progress in changes noted by Carroll Reed. In the contemporary period, Washington English also distinguishes itself from its California and Canadian neighbors. So, while we do not see a system-wide set of unique vowel qualities that are as vividly emblazoned on the public imagination as, for example, those of Southern US English(es), we do see a constellation of distinguishing features that yield an overall configuration that is something special. So, yes, folks, there is something to see here!

References

Assmann, P., and W. Katz. 2000. "Time-Varying Spectral Change in the Vowels of Children and Adults." *Journal of the Acoustical Society of America* 108:1856–1866.

Benson, Erica J., Michael J. Fox, and Jared Balkman. 2011. "The Bag That Scott Bought: The Low Vowels in Northwest Wisconsin." *American Speech* 86 (3): 271–311.

Boberg, Charles. 2005. "The Canadian Shift in Montreal." *Language Variation and Change* 17 (2): 133–154.

Clopper, C. G., D. B. Pisoni, and K. de Jong. 2005. "Acoustic Characteristics of the Vowel Systems of Six Regional Varieties of American English." *Journal of the Acoustical Society of America* 118 (3): 1661–1676.

Daniels, Roger. 1997. "The Exile and Return of Seattle's Japanese." *Pacific Northwest Quarterly* 88 (4): 166–173.

Eckert, Penelope. 2005. "California Vowels." http://www.stanford.edu/~eckert/vowels.html.

Freeman, Valerie. 2014. Bag, Beg, Bagel: Prevelar Raising and Merger in the Pacific Northwest English. General examination paper presented in partial fulfillment of the requirements of PhD, University of Washington, Seattle.

Fridland, Valerie, Tyler Kendall, Betsy Evans, and Alicia Wassink, eds. 2018. *Speech in the Western States: The Mountain West.* Volume 2 of Publications of the American Dialect Society. Durham, NC: Duke University Press.

Gamboa, Erasmo. 1981. "Mexican Migration into Washington State, A History, 1940–1950." *Pacific Northwest Quarterly* 72 (3): 121–131.

Hagiwara, Robert. 1997. "Dialect Variation and Formant Frequency: The American English Vowels Revisited." *Journal of the Acoustical Society of America* 102 (1): 655–658.

Labov, William, Sharon Ash, and Charles Boberg. 2006. *The Atlas of North American English: Phonetics, Phonology, and Sound Change.* New York: Mouton de Gruyter.

Ladefoged, Peter. 2005. *Vowels and Consonants.* Malden, MA: Wiley-Blackwell.

Lee, Everett S. 1957. *Population Redistribution and Economic Growth, United States, 1870–1950,* vol. 1, *Methodological Consideration and Reference Tables.* Philadelphia: American Philosophical Society.

Lemieux, Alice. 2005. Pacific Northwest Dialect Study: Vancouver WA Pilot Study. Undergraduate honors thesis, University of Washington.

Lieberman, Philip. 1977. *Speech Physiology and Acoustic Phonetics.* London: Macmillan.

Meany, Edmond S. 1946. *History of the State of Washington.* New York: MacMillan.

Mills, Carl. 1980. "The Sociolinguistics of the [a]-[b] Merger in Pacific Northwest English: A Subjective Reaction Test." *International Journal of Human Communication* 13 (2): 345–388.

Miyamoto, S. Frank. 1963. "The Japanese Minority in the Pacific Northwest." *Pacific Northwest Quarterly* 54 (4): 143–149.

Reed, Carroll. 1952. "The Pronunciation of English in the State of Washington." *American Speech* 27 (3):186–189.

Reed, Carroll. 1957. "Word Geography of the Pacific Northwest." *Orbis* 6:86–93.

Reed, Carroll. 1961. "The Pronunciation of English in the Pacific Northwest." *Language* 37 (4): 559–564.

Reed, Carroll. 1965. *Linguistic Atlas of the Pacific Northwest* (LAPNW). Athens: University of Georgia Library, Special Collections repository.

Reed, Carroll. 1983. "Linguistic Backpacking in the Pacific Northwest." *Journal of English Linguistics* 16 (1): 78–80.

Reiff, J. 1981. Urbanization and the Social Structure: Seattle, Washington 1852–1910. PhD diss., University of Washington, Seattle.

Riebold, John M. 2015. The Social Distribution of a Regional Change: /æg, ɛg, eg/ in Washington State. PhD diss., University of Washington, Seattle.

Sale, Roger. 1976. *Seattle Past to Present: An Interpretation of the History of the Foremost City in the Pacific Northwest.* Seattle: University of Washington Press.

Taylor, Quintard. 2003. *The Forging of a Black Community: Seattle's Central District from 1870 through the Civil Rights Era.* 3rd ed. Seattle: University of Washington Press.

Wassink, Alicia B. 2015. "Sociolinguistic Patterns in Seattle English." *Language Variation and Change* 27:1–28.

Wassink, Alicia B. 2017. "The Vowels of Washington State." In *Speech in the Western States: The Coastal States,* edited by Valerie Fridland, Tyler Kendall, Alicia Wassink, and Betsy Evans, 77–105. Publications of the American Dialect Society. Durham, NC: Duke University Press.

Wolfram, Walt, and Natalie Schilling. 2015. *American English: Dialects and Variation.* Oxford: Blackwell.

Yakama Nation Cultural Center. 2015. "Yakama History." http://www.yakamamuseum.com/home-history.php.

7

Seattle to Spokane
What Washingtonians Think about English Spoken in Their State

BETSY EVANS

In this chapter I discuss perceptions held by speakers in the Pacific Northwest (PNW) about the English that they and those around them use. This discussion draws largely on research conducted in Washington State but also includes other studies from around the region. It is commonplace for people to ask why linguists might be interested in the perceptions that speakers have about their language. In fact, the perceptions held by speakers in a community reflect many of the social discourses that are salient for them, and these can have important consequences for the growth or development of regional languages or dialects. By *social discourses* we mean common or frequent themes that are associated with people or things and how those themes are discussed by people; in this case, it especially refers to the way people talk about language and talk about people using the language. People's perceptions about language can be captured in many ways: some methods ask people to respond to audio recordings of different dialects; other methods involve asking people directly what they think about different dialects. In this way, linguists collect metalanguage, that is, the language used to talk about language. In this chapter we discuss a method to elicit people's perceptions about different dialects that involves asking people to indicate on a map where they think people speak differently. Then, the participants indicate whether they know any label or name for that way of speaking. This method was pioneered in sociolinguistics by Dennis Preston (1989), and this type of research is called perceptual dialectology (PD). PD is an important part of describing language, including the language of the PNW, because metalanguage can reveal what linguistic features speakers notice most often and also the attitudes held about the users of this language. As Niedzielski and Preston note, "Overt folk notions of geographical variation, based on neither production nor responses to forms, provide a helpful corollary to both production and attitude studies" (2003, 41). Information on attitudes to language variation can also provide linguists with perspectives on the future of a particular dialect or language (e.g., Indigenous languages in the PNW) and help linguists understand the process of language change (e.g., highly stigmatized linguistic features may fade away).

Opinions about language reflect beliefs about the speakers and their culture. That is, language itself cannot be lazy, slow, posh, and so on—these are features that listeners and speakers connect to a particular way of speaking. So, for example, if people believe the English in eastern Washington sounds "country," then "country" is likely a characteristic also connected to the people or culture of Eastern Washington (whether it's factually true or not) rather than a linguistic feature of the English. From a linguist's point of view, it means that there might be some language features that listeners notice in Eastern Washington, and therefore they connect it to the people and/or culture there. It is also important to note that respondents don't need firsthand experience with the groups they evaluate. As Hinton (2000, 156) explains, much of our "social knowledge" is created through communication within our own social groups without being informed by actual experience. This helps us understand why we might have perceptions about dialects that we've never personally encountered.

As described in other chapters in this book, the PNW has a very recent settlement history. The settlement patterns, combined with the fact that much linguistic research about US regional variation has concentrated on the eastern part of the United States, has resulted in a lack of descriptions of PNW English in the literature. In terms of perceptions of dialects, one thing we do know is that PNW English isn't noticeably different to people living in other parts of the United States. Some regions of the west, especially California, are places where some people living in other parts of the United States notice people as speaking differently (Preston 1989). Research surveying perceptions of English conducted on a national scale has shown that Washington (and the PNW) is associated with positive attributes such as "pleasant" and "standard" English (e.g., Preston 1989; Fridland and Bartlett 2006). Some Washingtonians in this study described Washington English as not noticeably different, whereas others mentioned features that may not be typically associated with English in Washington by Americans from other parts of the country, such as "country" or "Spanglish." Perceptions of variation of one's own dialect are complex and can differ from others' perceptions of that same dialect (Johnstone and Baumgardt 2004; Johnstone, Andrus and Danielson 2006; Johnstone and Kiesling 2008). Bucholtz et al. (2007) found that some stereotypes held nationally about California English (e.g., the Valley girl stereotype) were not mentioned when Californians described their own state's English. That is, Bucholtz et al. (2007) and Fought (2002) found that Californians themselves do not characterize their own English in the same way as outsiders do (nor do Washingtonians, as we will see below).

In Oregon, Hartley conducted a PD map study and found that Oregonians identified Washington and Oregon as distinct and as the most "correct" English among the fifty US states (1999, 321). A few (16/66) even drew a region they labeled as "Pacific Northwest" on their maps (322). One distinction that the Oregonian respondents made between Oregon and Washington was on the scale of "pleasantness." As noted in Becker, too (this volume), Oregonians rated Oregon English as more pleasant than Washington English (323). Because Oregonians rated Oregon English as distinct but also very "correct" and "pleasant," Hartley (1999, 323) suggests that these respondents possess "linguistic security," a feeling of confidence that their language is standard (this concept is described in more detail below). Below, the notion of linguistic security is discussed with regard to Washingtonians, and we will see that they also possess some degree of linguistic security.

WHAT DO WASHINGTONIANS THINK?

Here we go into more detail about what Washingtonians think about English in their state by describing a perceptual dialectology map study conducted there (Evans 2011, 2013a, 2013b, 2016). The perceptions of Washingtonians certainly do not represent all residents of the PNW but their perceptions are a result of their experience as residents of the PNW and help us understand some aspects of Northwest voices.

In this study, perceptions of English in Washington were collected via the hand-drawn map technique (Preston 1989) from 229 Washington residents who were given paper copies of maps of Washington. Respondents were asked to "draw a line around places where you think people's English sounds different. Next, write down what you'd call that way of talking, if you can think of a label for it." Figure 7.1 is an example of a map drawn by

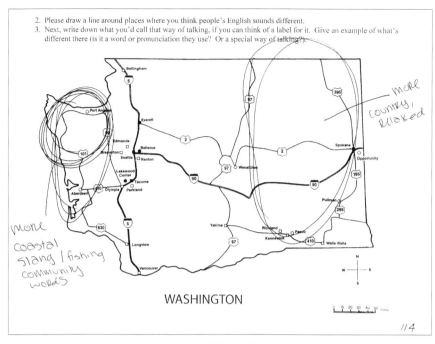

2. Please draw a line around places where you think people's English sounds different.
3. Next, write down what you'd call that way of talking, if you can think of a label for it. Give an example of what's different there (is it a word or pronunciation they use? Or a special way of talking?)

WASHINGTON

Fig. 7.1. Map drawn by a twenty-one-year-old female from Western Washington.

a respondent. Each respondent's paper map was analyzed using a sophisticated digital process that involved tracing all the lines on the maps. Once all the lines were digitized, they could be combined to create a composite map showing where all the respondents drew lines (for more on the methodology, see Evans 2013b).

Figure 7.2 is the product of the analysis of the 178 maps with lines drawn on them. It shows consistent patterns of perception of spatial differentiation among English speakers in Washington. First, a large number of respondents indicated that Eastern Washington is a place where English is "different." Second, urban areas all over the state and Eastern Washington in general were areas where respondents indicated that people speak "differently." A few respondents even referred to specific linguistic patterns that have been only recently described by linguists (e.g., Wassink, this volume). This is especially interesting in light of the lack of data on the English of this region. The details of these results are described below.

In addition to the creation of composite maps, the labels written on the maps were also examined via a content analysis (Bauer 2000). The majority of the labels (n=336) were associated with a shape drawn on the map. Labels that were made on the map without any other marking on the map, such

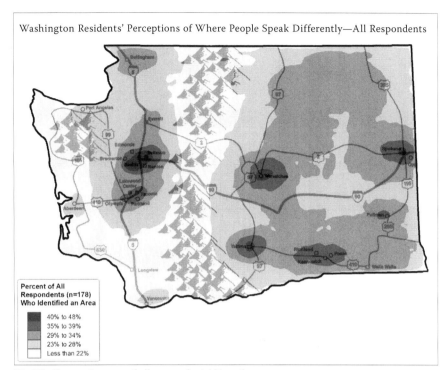

Washington Residents' Perceptions of Where People Speak Differently—All Respondents

Percent of All
Respondents (n=178)
Who Identified an Area

40% to 48%
35% to 39%
29% to 34%
23% to 28%
Less than 22%

Fig. 7.2. Composite map of all respondents' lines drawn on maps.

as "all the same" (n=31), were not included in the map analysis (see Evans 2013a). The content analysis procedure examines the content of each label in order to group similar labels. Common themes in the data can emerge as words and phrases are collated with others in the same semantic field. For example, *southern* and *cowboy* were combined to form one category called "country." If more than one different word or phrase was associated with a single shape on the map, each one was considered as a separate response. So, a single shape with more than one label (from the same respondent), such as "Mostly newscaster, Spanglish," would result in two categories associated with that shape on the map: "standard" and "Spanish." The content analysis resulted in twenty categories. The categories that the most labels fit into were "country" (25 percent of all labels) and "Spanish" (12 percent of all labels). Although this method of analysis of keywords does allow for some respondents' opinions to be overrepresented (e.g., one respondent gives more labels than others), selecting only one label for a shape that has several labels means that some of the respondents' perceptions are not represented. If the labels are grouped into categories, a variety of types of maps of labels can also be created (Evans 2016).

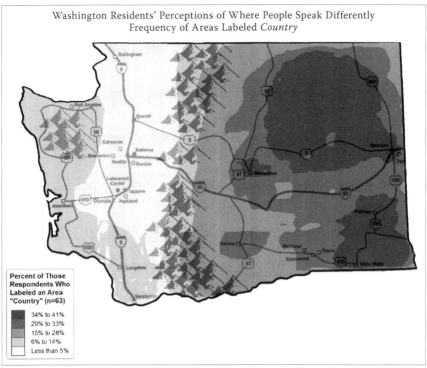

Washington Residents' Perceptions of Where People Speak Differently
Frequency of Areas Labeled *Country*

Percent of Those
Respondents Who
Labeled an Area
"Country" (n=63)

34% to 41%
29% to 33%
15% to 28%
6% to 14%
Less than 5%

Fig. 7.3. Composite map of regions labeled "country."

MAJOR THEMES: COUNTRY

The most frequent labels (86/336 or 25 percent) related to notions of
rural life and were most frequently associated with regions in Eastern
Washington. This category of labels, called "country," comprises labels
such as "hick," "farmer talk," and "country." Figure 7.3 is a composite
map showing the spatial representation of the "country" category. In the
case of country, sixty-three respondents marked a "country" label on the
Washington map. Because a single respondent may have used a "country"
label for more than one shape they drew on the map, there are eighty-six
locations on the map with a "country" label. In order for the map to be
easily interpretable, the percentage of respondents who used such a label
is represented.

The darkest areas in these maps indicate where the most overlap
occurs. For example, the darkest area in figure 7.3 represents the overlap
of up to 41 percent of the respondents' answers (for all maps, groupings of
different color values were selected to reflect the most visually descriptive
representation of the data). Figure 7.3 shows that the majority of the region

east of the Cascades is associated with "country" labels. In addition, up to 14 percent of the respondents in this category associate the Pacific coastline with "country." It may not seem surprising that Eastern Washington is attributed with such a label, given the high percentage of rural communities in that area (WWAMI Rural Health Research Center 2005). However, this result raises the question of what leads respondents to use the words like "country" to describe language there.

We think it might be the case that Eastern Washington is salient in this way for linguistic, geographic, and sociocultural reasons. First, as described above, Eastern Washington was settled by a number of US Midlands dialect speakers. Some linguistic features from the Midlands may exist in Eastern Washington. There is anecdotal attestation in Eastern Washington of Midlands features such as tensing of lax vowels before voiced fricatives (e.g., *innovative* as something like "inn-uh-vay-teev," *pleasure* as "play-zure") and intrusive /r/ (e.g., "Warshington"), both Midlands features (Thomas 2001, 84, for the former; Pederson 2001, 272, for the latter). These features of English of the US Midlands are often perceived as nonstandard and Southern-sounding by people from north and west of that region, as the region possesses some features associated with southern US English (Murray and Simon 2006). That is to say, Washingtonians may be hearing some linguistic features brought from the Midlands to Eastern Washington and perceive them to be "southern" or possibly "rural."

Second, there are, quite literally, farmers in Eastern Washington. The nature of the terrain in the counties in this region means that its economic and cultural emphases are different than those in western counties of Washington; these counties are the top agricultural producers in the state (Washington State Department of Agriculture 2007). The terrain of Eastern Washington also has provided very suitable conditions for raising livestock. By the mid-nineteenth century in the Pacific Northwest "the cattle industry boomed" (Galbraith and Anderson 1991, 13). Galbraith and Anderson note, "It is important to the history of the great American West to recognize the contribution made by the cattle industry of the Pacific Northwest" (1991, 214). The workers associated with this industry—cattlemen, stockmen, and cowboys—are the origin of the rodeos in the region. In the mid-nineteenth century, roundups were held for counting and branding cattle and assessing the herd, but they also served the purpose of cowboys meeting with others and staging impromptu competitions, including "horse racing, roping, and bronco riding contests among the working cowboys" (Allen 1998, 70). According to Allen, the roundup activity developed into something more organized and, "by the early 1920s, cowboys on at least two Kittitas valley ranches were staging regular contests or, as the locals called them 'Sunday rodeos'" (1998, 71). Therefore the perception among respondents that there are cowboys in Eastern Washington has its roots in the history of the region. This point is connected to the third reason that respondents may perceive Eastern Washington as "country." There seems to be some commercial value in cultivating an aura of country in the region, and this cultivation of "country" is not new for Eastern Washington. A renowned rodeo in Ellensburg, Washington, was started in 1923, and according to Allen (1998),

> The Ellensburg Rodeo was more commercial than a truly folkloric roundup, ranch rodeo or even a Sunday rodeo. It certainly was not a direct offshoot of pioneer cattle frontier lifestyle, for by 1923 there was very little of that lifestyle left; the Kittitas Valley frontier had vanished two generations earlier. (73)

Omak (northeast Washington) is a town that has hosted an annual rodeo since 1933 (called the Omak Stampede). The Stampede is capitalized on by a variety of businesses in town such as the Stampede Hotel, Stampede Mini Market, and Stampede Teriyaki restaurant. The Toppenish Chamber of Commerce (located in south-central Washington) provides another example of this capitalization on the local cultural activity. On their website they proclaim "We're the BEST OF THE WEST!" and proudly inform the visitor that "Toppenish was named a Must-See Old West Destination by True West Magazine in 2010" (http://www.toppenish.net/). The appearance of the website also has a western theme (e.g., typeface, color, embellishments). These are only a few examples, but it seems apparent that some communities in Eastern Washington actively cultivate the rodeo/cowboy culture.

In summary, a perception of "country" may be associated with Eastern Washington because of possible linguistic features, successful agricultural economy, and the cultivation of "country" culture in some communities.

MAJOR THEME: EAST VERSUS WEST

Related to the evaluation of Eastern Washington as different is a sense among Washington residents that Eastern and Western Washington are

sociopolitically dissimilar and, in some ways, at odds. This is demonstrated by the fact that residents refer to the Cascade Range that crosses
the state from north to south as the "Cascade curtain." Thus it serves as a
literal and figurative line that divides the state. Figures 7.4 and 7.5 compare the responses from eastern and western residents to explore how
residents' Eastern or Western Washington origins might influence their
perception of language around the state. For these maps, respondents
were grouped according to the location of their hometown. Figure 7.4
shows a composite map of the responses from respondents from Eastern
Washington (n=103). Figure 7.5 is a map of the responses from respondents from Western Washington (n=75). A comparison of figures 7.4 and
7.5 shows that Eastern and Western Washington respondents agree on
several urban areas that are places where people speak differently. They
also agree that Eastern Washington is a place where people speak differently. However, the percentage of eastern versus western respondents
who identified Eastern Washington is slightly different. A smaller percentage of Eastern Washingtonians (16–30 percent) marked the region
of Eastern Washington as different, whereas 41–45 percent of western
Washingtonians marked it as different. In addition, figure 7.4 shows that,
for Eastern Washingtonians, difference in Eastern Washington is less
differentiated and is concentrated in the center of Eastern Washington.
Eastern Washingtonian respondents also indicated more differentiation
in the Seattle area in comparison to the western respondents. This may
suggest that Eastern Washingtonians do not view their own region as very
different, or do not view it as different as Western Washingtonians do.
As described above, the perceived sociopolitical divide and the "country"
theme associated with Eastern Washington is likely driving this perception of difference for all Washingtonians.

Broad undifferentiated marking on the map by respondents may
signal a lack of distinguishing linguistic features that are salient to these
respondents (even if this is only a perception). In the US context, "standard" dialects are usually those that are considered to have no characteristics that are stigmatized. When a community or speaker feels sure
that their dialect is "standard," linguists refer to this feeling as "linguistic
security" (Labov 1966; Trudgill 1972). Linguistic security is often found
in speech communities that are not stigmatized. Preston (1989) found
that respondents in southeast Michigan (a region with few linguistic
stereotypes) rated their own English as the most correct in the United

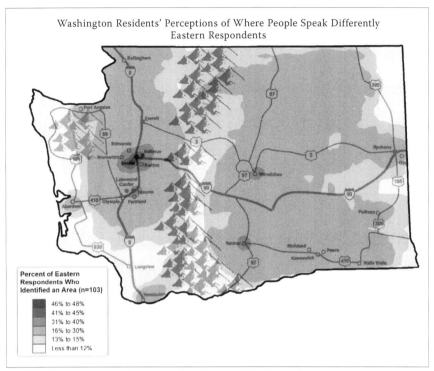

Fig. 7.4. Composite map of responses from Eastern Washingtonians.

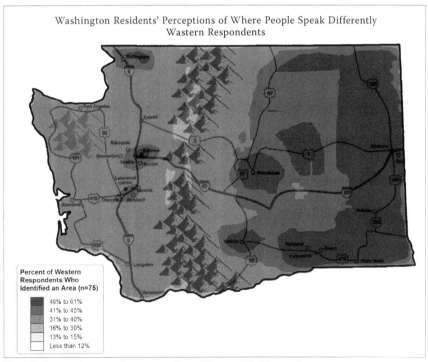

Fig. 7.5. Composite map of responses from Western Washingtonians.

States, whereas Southerners (a region with many linguistic stereotypes) rated their English as less correct than several other US regions. Recall that Hartley (1999) found evidence of linguistic security in her research in Oregon. In fact, a few respondents from both Eastern and Western Washington labeled their own variety as "normal." "Normal" in this case very likely indicates "lacking any non-standard features" (Niedzielski and Preston 2003). Given that Western Washington respondents indicated larger regions in the east as different (figure 7.5), it isn't too surprising to find labels of "normal," or standardness, attributed to Western Washington by western residents. For example, an eighteen-year-old male from Seattle labeled the whole of Western Washington as "people that talk normally and pronounce things properly." Similar labels were given by other western residents to Western Washington, such as "regular" and "normal English" (a nineteen-year-old female from Seattle). It is interesting, however, to find what looks like linguistic security among Eastern Washington speakers as well. Because many respondents perceived difference in that region and also frequently labeled that region as "country" or "southern," we might expect the dialect there to be maligned, because these are labels that often correlate with negative status for a language variety in the United States (Niedzielski and Preston 2003; but see Hall-Lew and Stephens 2012 for other associations). Comments from Eastern Washingtonians suggest a perception that Eastern Washington is also a place where standard English is used. For example, a female respondent from Eastern Washington indicated that her own region is "mostly newscaster" and labeled a large region surrounding Seattle as "Most speak like newscasters (like in central [Washington])." A few other respondents from Eastern Washington indicated positive evaluation of their own variety, such as "normal." For example, a twenty-three year-old female from Eastern Washington labeled her own town as "normal" but the region west of it as "farmer, hickish" (figure 7.6). An eighteen-year-old male from Central Washington labeled the middle section of Eastern Washington extending to Spokane as "normal English." And a nineteen-year-old-male from Wenatchee labeled his own town and Yakima (to the south) as "standard." This apparent linguistic security in Eastern Washington suggests the possibility of a "regional standard."

That is to say, Eastern Washingtonians perceive the English that they use to be correct and are unaware that the variety is perceived by outsiders (Western Washingtonians) as different (see also Sandoval, this volume).

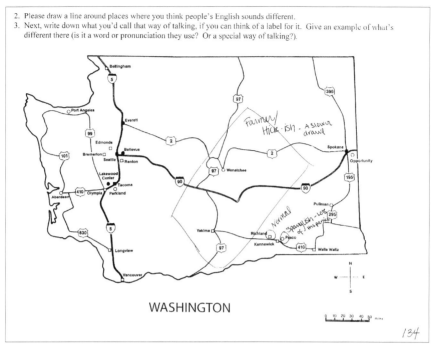

2. Please draw a line around places where you think people's English sounds different.
3. Next, write down what you'd call that way of talking, if you can think of a label for it. Give an example of what's different there (is it a word or pronunciation they use? Or a special way of talking?).

Fig. 7.6. Map drawn by a twenty-three-year-old female from Eastern Washington.

Hartley suggests, "It may be that the traditional categories of linguistic security/insecurity do not apply in the same way in western states, where a multiplicity and therefore awareness of distinctive dialects is not as prevalent as in eastern and southern states" (1999, 323). Thus the typical patterns of perceptual attributes regarding linguistic security/insecurity (Niedzielski and Preston 2003) may not be found in western states because of the emerging development of linguistic stereotypes resulting from its more recent settlement history by comparison to the eastern United States (see Battistella and Pippin, this volume, for more on settlement patterns).

MAJOR THEME: SPANISH

Labels like "Spanglish," "spanish [*sic*] influence," and "Mexenglish" form the second largest category (12 percent) of labels called "Spanish." Figure 7.7 shows the regions that respondents circled and gave a label that fit the category "Spanish." Labels that fit the category "Spanglish" were largely attributed to regions in Eastern Washington—Wenatchee, Yakima, and the Tri-Cities (Kennewick, Pasco, and Richland). The populations of these

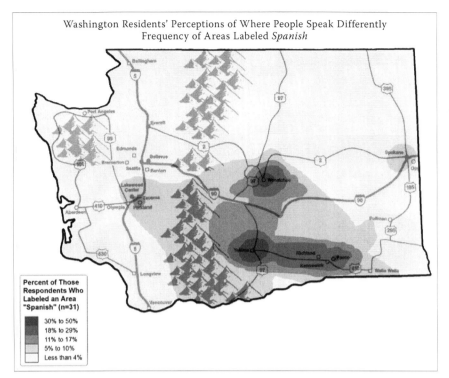

Washington Residents' Perceptions of Where People Speak Differently
Frequency of Areas Labeled *Spanish*

Percent of Those Respondents Who Labeled an Area "Spanish" (n=31)

30% to 50%
18% to 29%
11% to 17%
5% to 10%
Less than 4%

Fig. 7.7. Composite map of regions labeled as "Spanish."

regions are up to 50 percent Hispanic (Washington State Office of Financial Management 2010. This population distribution is partly a result of migration of Mexicans to the Yakima Valley after World War II (Gamboa 1981); however Latinx people have been present in the Washington region since before Washington became a state in 1889. This population may account for the perception of an influence of Spanish there. Without interviewing the respondents, it's impossible to determine what the influence of Spanish in that region means to them. That is, we don't know if their perception of this population distribution is positive or negative based solely on the labels and categories.

OTHER NOTABLE THEMES

Some respondents indicated that there are no differences in the English spoken in Washington, suggesting a belief that English is homogeneous in Washington. For example, a sixty-one-year-old male from Seattle simply wrote on his map, "I haven't noticed any obvious differences in the way people talk in Wash. State." Another respondent, an eighteen-year-old

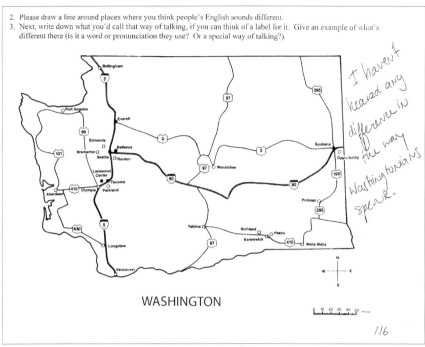

2. Please draw a line around places where you think people's English sounds different.
3. Next, write down what you'd call that way of talking, if you can think of a label for it. Give an example of what's different there (is it a word or pronunciation they use? Or a special way of talking?).

WASHINGTON

I haven't heard any difference in the way Washingtonians speak.

116

Fig. 7.8. Map drawn by an eighteen-year-old female from Seattle.

woman from Seattle, wrote, "I haven't heard any differences in the way Washingtonians speak" (figure 7.8). This perception was indicated by a small subset of the entire data set of 229 respondents described above (see Evans 2013a). (See Becker, this volume, for recent results from Oregon that also indicate perceptions of linguistic homogeneity.) These results suggest that linguistic differences may go unnoticed (or ignored) by some speakers who are linguistically secure.

The labels that are not present in the data are also informative as a way of understanding what is *not* salient to respondents. Because of the historical and continued presence of Indigenous people in Washington State, one might expect to see respondents indicating on their maps the influence of Indigenous languages or culture on how English is different around the state. However, such comments were very few. Only 6/229 respondents marked a label on their map that referred to Indigenous peoples' influence, such as "rez talk" or "tribal." An absence of the influence of Indigenous people on perceptions of Washington English may reflect a lack of interaction of respondents with the Indigenous populations.

WHAT WE LEARN FROM PERCEPTUAL DIALECTOLOGY IN WASHINGTON ABOUT LANGUAGE AND CULTURE IN THE PACIFIC NORTHWEST

It's important to remember, as described above, that expressions about a language variety reflect the perceptions held about the individuals or groups associated with that variety rather than factors held within language itself. The feelings that listeners have about a variety are directly linked to the feelings they have about the speakers. The composite maps created from these respondents' own maps indicate that the majority perceive the English of Eastern Washington to be notably different. Respondents suggest that it is a place where there are many farmers and Latinos, all of whom sound "different." Labels for those regions (e.g., "hick," "country talk") also suggest respondents believe "nonstandard" speech is used there. Standard language ideology, the belief that there is a "correct" and "proper" way to use a language (Lippi-Green 2012, 67), is strongly suggested in the responses. Respondents pay much attention to where "normal"/standard and nonstandard English are spoken. This is consistent with previous PD research, as described by Preston, who has argued that, when non-linguists are asked about difference, "the primary consideration is correct-ness" (1989, 71).

Unlike other parts of the United States, where regional dialect features are very salient (e.g., the South, New York City), the PNW is not a region with a notably different dialect, in general, for outsiders and even for some Washington residents. In addition, the PNW is a place where linguistic security predominates, especially in comparison to some other US regions (Sandoval, this volume; Niedzielski and Preston 2003), even in regions of Washington that all respondents agreed are "different." The perception and actual production of linguistic difference is usually connected to sig-nificant social differences between communities. In the PNW, the lack of noticeable features and linguistic security can be partly attributed to the nature of the settlement of the region (see Battistella and Pippin, this vol-ume; Richardson, this volume; Wassink, this volume), a settlement pattern that did not lend itself to the development of ethnic enclaves (Rieff 1981). Thus, with a few exceptions, Washington State has not experienced the same local oppositional identities as other regions in the United States. The result, for language variation, is that the social differences of the communities in contact that have generated linguistic difference in other parts of the United States (Wolfram and Schilling 2016) are not so large or important in the PNW such that they have generated noticeable linguistic differences. This seems to be especially true for those outside of the region, who don't perceive linguistic difference at all in the PNW. However, on the local level, for Washington residents, linguistic differences in some regions of Washington are noticeable because of the social and cultural differences or urban/rural differences that are apparent only to residents of the state.

References

Allen, Michael. 1998. "Real Cowboys? The Origins and Evolution of North American Rodeo and Rodeo Cowboys." *Journal of the West* 37 (1): 69–79.

Bauer, Martin W. 2000. "Classical Content Analysis: A Review." In *Qualitative Researching with Text, Image and Sound: A Practical Handbook*, edited by Martin W. Bauer and George Gaskell, 131–151. London: Sage.

Bucholtz, Mary, Nancy Bermudez, Victor Fung, Lisa Edwards, and Rosalva Vargas. 2007. "Hella Nor Cal or Totally So Cal? The Perceptual Dialectology of California." *Journal of English Linguistics* 35 (4): 325–352.

Evans, Betsy E. 2011. "Seattletonian to Faux Hick: Mapping Perceptions of English in WA." *American Speech* 86 (4): 383–413.

Evans, Betsy E. 2013a. "'Everybody Sounds the Same': Otherwise Invisible Ideology in Perceptual Dialectology." *American Speech* 88 (1): 62–80.

Evans, Betsy E. 2013b. "Seattle to Spokane: Mapping Perceptions of English in Washington State." *Journal of English Linguistics* 41 (3): 268–291.

Evans, Betsy, E. 2016. "City Talk and Country Talk: Perceptions of Urban and Rural English in Washington State." In *Cityscapes and Perceptual Dialectology: Global Perspectives on Non-Linguists' Knowledge of the Dialect Landscape*, edited by Jennifer Cramer and Christopher Montgomery. Berlin: Mouton de Gruyter.

Fought, Carmen. 2002. "California Students' Perceptions of, You Know, Regions and Dialects?" In *Handbook of Perceptual Dialectology*, vol. 2, edited by Daniel Long and Dennis R. Preston, 113–134. Amsterdam: Benjamins.

Fridland, Valerie, and Kathryn Bartlett. 2006. "Correctness, Pleasantness, and Degree of Difference Ratings across Regions." *American Speech* 81 (4): 358–386.

Galbraith, William A., and E. William Anderson. 1991 [1971]. "Grazing History of the Northwest." *Rangelands* 13 (5): 213–218. Reprinted from *Journal of Range Management* 24 (1): 6–12.

Gamboa, Erasmo. 1981. "Mexican Migration into Washington State: A History, 1940–1950." *Pacific Northwest Quarterly* 72 (3): 121–131.

Hall-Lew, Lauren, and Nola Stephens. 2012. "Country Talk." *Journal of English Linguistics* 40 (3): 256–280.

Hartley, Laura C. 1999. "A View from the West: Perceptions of U.S. Dialects by Oregon Residents." In *Handbook of Perceptual Dialectology*, vol. 1, edited by Dennis Preston, 315–332. Amsterdam: Benjamins.

Hinton, Perry R. 2000. *Stereotypes, Cognition and Culture*. Hove, UK: Psychology Press.

Johnstone, Barbara, and Dan Baumgardt. 2004. "'Pittsburghese' Online: Vernacular Norming in Conversation." *American Speech* 79 (2): 115–145.

Johnstone, Barbara, and Scott F. Kiesling. 2008. "Indexicality and Experience: Exploring the Meanings of /aw/-monophthongization in Pittsburgh." *Journal of Sociolinguistics* 12 (1): 5–33.

Johnstone, Barbara, Jennifer Andrus, and Andrew E. Danielson. 2006. "Mobility, Indexicality, and the Enregisterment of 'Pittsburghese.'" *Journal of English Linguistics* 34 (2): 77–104.

Labov, William. 1966. *The Social Stratification of English in New York City*. Washington, DC: Center for Applied Linguistics.

Lippi-Green, Rosina. 2012. *English with an Accent*. 2nd ed. New York: Routledge.

Milroy, James, and Lesley Milroy. 1999. *Authority in Language: Investigating Standard English*. London: Routledge.

Murray, Thomas E., and Beth Lee Simon, eds. 2006. *Language Variation and Change in the American Midland: A New Look at "Heartland" English*. Amsterdam: Benjamins.

Niedzielski, Nancy A., and Dennis R. Preston. 2003. *Folk Linguistics*. Berlin: Mouton de Gruyter.

Pederson, Lee. 2001. "Dialects." In *The Cambridge History of the English Language*, edited by Richard M. Hogg, vol. 6, *English in North America*, edited by John Algeo, 253–290. Cambridge: Cambridge University Press.

Preston, Dennis R. 1989. *Perceptual Dialectology*. Dordrecht: Foris.

Reiff, J. 1981. Urbanization and the Social Structure: Seattle, Washington 1852–1910. PhD diss., University of Washington, Seattle.

Thomas, Erik. 2001. *An Acoustic Analysis of Vowel Variation in New World English*. Publication of the American Dialect Society 85. Durham, NC: Duke University Press.

Trudgill, Peter. 1972. "Sex, Covert Prestige and Linguistic Change in the Urban British English of Norwich." *Language in Society* 1 (2): 179–195.

Washington State Department of Agriculture. 2007. "Top Crops and Food Processing Industries." http://agr.wa.gov/AgInWa/Crop_Maps.aspx.

Washington State Office of Financial Management. 2010. "Hispanics: April 1, 2010 Population Estimates." http://www.ofm.wa.gov/pop/race/minoritygraphics/hispanic10.pdf.

Wolfram, Walt, and Natalie Schilling. 2016. *American English: Dialects and Variation*. Malden, MA: John Wiley and Sons.

WWAMI Rural Health Research Center. 2005. "Rural-Urban Commuting Area Codes (RUCA) Data." http://depts.washington.edu/uwruca/ruca-data.php.

8

What Oregon English Can Tell Us about Dialect Diversity in the Pacific Northwest

KARA BECKER

In studies of language in use, scholars distinguish between *production* (what speakers *say*) and *perception* (what speakers *think* about language). When it comes to a regional dialect, production studies describe the distinctive linguistic features that mark speakers as from some place. In American English, these distinctive features are most numerous at the level of phonology, or the sound system; for example, speakers from New York City produce the vowel in words like *coffee* in a distinctive way, with the first vowel rounded and raised so it sounds like "cawfee." By describing these kinds of features and how they pattern across regions, as well as within regions across different social groups, dialectologists are able to identify and label distinct dialects. In addition to production studies, more and more scholarship is incorporating perceptual data into research on American regional dialects. The term perception is broad, but generally refers to how speakers react to linguistic information; this can be in the form of basic social evaluations ("This person sounds like they're from the South") to more established beliefs or *language ideologies* ("People from the South sound lazy and uneducated"). Importantly, we now know that production and perception are intimately connected—the patterning of linguistic features in production provides the material for speakers' evaluations, attitudes, and ideologies in perception, and speakers' language ideologies can influence language production, in a continuous feedback loop.

This chapter explores the notion that the Pacific Northwest is a unified dialect region using data from both production and perception from native speakers of Oregon English. Until recently, there has been very little research on dialects in the Pacific Northwest, with the general consensus from both lay speakers and dialectologists that there is not a distinctive

PNW dialect. However, a growing body of research provides concrete evidence that speech in the PNW is distinctive. Whether the regional patterns warrant a label of "PNW English," though, is not clear, making contemporary data from Oregon natives crucial to delineating dialect diversity in the Northwest. As outlined in this chapter, evidence from Oregon speakers' production finds a number of distinctive features, but does not necessarily support a picture of a cohesive PNW dialect region. Oregonians produce a feature characteristic of the PNW, BAG and BEG tensing (discussed in Wassink, this volume), but they also participate in numerous widespread sound changes that link them to the West and North America more broadly. Crucially, these larger changes in progress have not been documented consistently in Washington State. In contrast, evidence from perception suggests that Oregonians see their language use as part of a Pacific Northwest region, and that they view this region in contrast to California. Combined, the two perspectives highlight the need to chart the continued diversification of English in the Pacific Northwest, where language use and language attitudes work together to affect language change.

THE BACKDROP: THE IDEOLOGY OF NON-ACCENT IN THE PNW

Ask a native resident of the Pacific Northwest, and they'll probably tell you confidently that they don't have an accent. This is actually not a common language ideology in the United States—speakers from the South, the Northeast, and elsewhere are very aware of their local dialect and can easily describe the way people talk where they are from (Preston 2002). Of course, linguists know that all speakers have accents, or regionally specific speech traits, which makes the "myth of non-accent" (Lippi-Green 1997) that characterizes some areas all the more interesting. What prompts speakers to view their own speech as unmarked and standard? First, a belief in non-accent suggests a high level of linguistic security, meaning that speakers generally feel good about the way that they talk. A study of Oregonians' language attitudes found that they rated the speech of Oregon and Washington highest of all the fifty states on scales of "correctness" and "pleasantness" (Hartley 1999), as noted in Evans (this volume). A belief in non-accent also suggests that the features distinctive to the region may be below the level of conscious awareness; that is, speakers just don't notice them. Indeed, this is likely the case for English in the Pacific Northwest, where speakers appear to be only just beginning to become aware of what marks their regional speech.

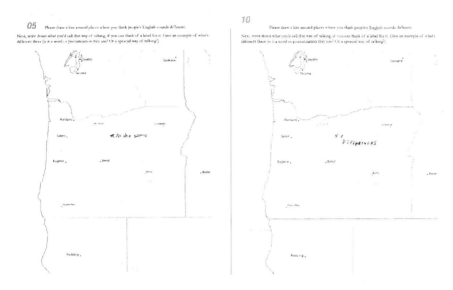

Fig. 8.1. Two map task responses demonstrating the common ideology of non-accent shared by many Oregonians.

Overall, the PNW dialect region is characterized by an "ideology of non-accent," or a belief in a homogeneous, accentless variety. In recent research (Becker et al. 2016), Oregonians were given a blank map of Oregon and parts of Washington, Idaho, and California and asked to "draw a line around places where you think people's English sounds different." This classic map task is a common tool in perceptual dialectology (Niedzielski and Preston 2003), and most speakers of American English have no problem filling in the map, drawing circles and lines around distinctive areas and providing colorful descriptors. Many Oregonians, in contrast, produced maps like the ones in figure 8.1. These speakers in effect declined to complete the task, asserting that they could not draw lines around distinctive areas on the map and instead noting that speech in the area is "all the same" or has "no differences." Residents of Washington State have also demonstrated the ideology of non-accent in similar map tasks (Evans 2013, and this volume).

Dialectologists have aligned with the perspective of everyday speakers that the PNW is lacking in dialect distinction. Compared to other dialect regions, the PNW has remained understudied, receiving little scholarly interest until very recently. The few studies that do exist have concluded that speech in the PNW was too variable to form a coherent region (Labov, Ash, and Boberg 2006). *The Atlas of North American English*, the major

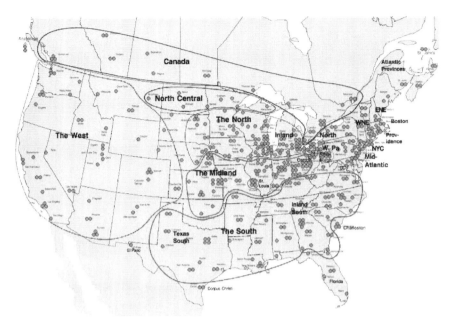

Fig. 8.2. The major North American dialect areas, including "The West," from Labov, Ash, and Boberg (2006).

contemporary dialect atlas, places the PNW into the massive and general "West" region (see figure 8.2) and concludes that this area is characterized by "a lack of homogeneity and uniqueness" (Labov, Ash, and Boberg 2006, 284). The reasons suggested for this lack of homogeneity have to do with the diverse history of settlement of the western states, which brought speakers from across the United States, including from the Northern, Midlands, and Southern dialect regions (Labov Ash, and Boberg 2006; Wassink 2015, and this volume).

The perspective from dialectologists that the PNW is too heterogeneous has contributed to the overall view of it as lacking in distinction—too much idiosyncratic individual variability blocks the formation of a distinctive dialect region. Interestingly, this conclusion in turn aligns with residents' view of homogeneity, because the lack of a bounded, notable dialect allows speakers to conclude that there simply is no PNW accent. And so the "no accent" that results from heterogeneity aligns with the "no accent" resulting from the homogeneity of the ideology of non-accent: because there is no regional accent, it must be the case that speakers use the unmarked American English standard.

This is the context for the recent surge in research on dialect use in the PNW. Lay speakers and scholars alike have overlooked the PNW, perceived as lacking in distinctive regional markers, and the ideology of non-accent remains a common belief of many residents of the area. Yet once dialectologists began to look more closely at speech in the PNW, it became clear there was more to the region than was previously described.

EVIDENCE FROM PRODUCTION: DIALECT DISTINCTION IN OREGON

The Atlas of North American English defines "the West" less by what it is than by what it is not. In short, the West lacks the contemporary distinctive features found in other regions. The *Atlas* does note that the West participates in some regional sound changes, specifically the low back merger of the vowel classes BOT and BOUGHT, which sound the same for westerners, and the fronting of the vowel class BOOT. However, these features are widespread across North America, so their presence in the West does little to enhance its dialect distinction. And beyond these features, the *Atlas* concludes that there is little else that marks the West as distinct.

In contrast to the *Atlas'* view of the West, recent scholarship along the West Coast has identified distinctive regional features. To the north of Oregon, in Washington State, scholars have identified a distinctive feature that they argue is characteristic of the PNW—the tensing of the vowels in BAG and BEG (Wassink 2015, and this volume). To the south, in California, much research has documented the California Vowel Shift, a rotation of the vowels in BIT, BET, BAT, and BOT, which is most likely a more widespread shift found in Canada and elsewhere across North America. The sections that follow define these features and outline their presence in the production of native speakers of Oregon English.

BAG AND BEG TENSING

Because all dialects mark regional information in phonology, or the sound system, the pronunciation of vowels is a rich area for descriptions of regional distinction in American English. Recent research in Washington State (Wassink 2015, and this volume) provides evidence of a distinctive PNW trait in the pronunciation of two vowels when pronounced before a /g/ sound. Words like *bag* and *tag* sound more like "beg" and "teg" in the PNW, and words like *beg* and *keg* sound more like "beyg" and "keyg." Phonetically, these vowels are "tensed," or produced in a more raised and fronted position in the vowel space. This feature is known as BAG and BEG tensing and has been well documented in Washington State (Freeman 2013; Wassink 2015).

The identification of BAG and BEG tensing is quite exciting, given the backdrop described above. First, dialectologists had little to say about the PNW and the West as a whole, so this research fills an important gap in describing local regional distinction in Washington State. Second, the ubiquity of the ideology of non-accent means that explanations that PNW residents actually *do* have accents will fall on deaf ears without linguists being able to point to a specific linguistic trait that marks the region. Additionally, many PNW residents do recognize BAG and BEG tensing as something they hear in the speech of local residents and, once it is pointed out, acknowledge that this feature marks the local language.

Because BAG and BEG tensing could be the first distinctive PNW feature to be described by dialectologists, it is crucial to have evidence from speaker production across the PNW region. Data from Oregonians' production demonstrates that residents from the state do indeed produce this feature. Words like *bag* and *beg* are produced significantly higher and fronter in the vowel space than words like *back* and *bet*, respectively (Becker et al. 2016). Combined with the research from Washington State, the evidence from Oregonians contributes to a picture of a PNW dialect region with BAG and BEG tensing as a defining feature.

However, evidence of how this feature patterns within groups of Oregon English complicates the view of BAG and BEG tensing in the PNW. In studies of language change, sociolinguists analyze patterns of use across age groups as a way to approximate change across time. If older speakers use a feature more than middle-aged speakers, who use it more than younger speakers, we can say that this feature is decreasing in use in a speech community. We can do this because the speech of older residents can be said to approximate the dialect as used during their youth, when our regional patterns are fixed, while the speech of middle-aged speakers approximates the dialect of *their* youth, and so on. In this way, contemporary data can be used to track language change in the absence of longitudinal data. For BAG and BEG tensing, some studies have found a pattern across age groups that suggests that this feature is receding over time; namely, the youngest speakers sampled produce this feature less than older speakers (Becker et al. 2016; Freeman 2013). If these findings are representative, then this distinctive PNW feature, only recently discovered, is in recession, and may no longer mark the region in the future.

The age pattern leads to a number of interesting questions regarding the role of BAG and BEG tensing as a defining feature of a PNW dialect. Is it really receding, and if so, where? Only more studies of production across the region can resolve these issues. Perhaps the feature will recede in some areas, like Portland, while maintaining a presence in others, serving to break up the PNW region into smaller dialect areas by state or city for this feature. If it is receding, will it be lost entirely, and cease to serve as a marker of PNW speech? Regardless of these outstanding questions, it is clear that language use in the PNW is not lacking in uniqueness, but instead is a resource that allows its residents to mark themselves as from the region.

THE SHORT FRONT VOWEL SHIFT

The presence of BAG and BEG tensing in the speech of both Oregonians and Washingtonians suggests that these two states might be members of a cohesive dialect region. However, it is also important to evaluate the rest of the vowel space to confirm that the overall systems of Oregonians and Washingtonians are similar. This is because our regional accents are rarely characterized by a single feature, but rather by a constellation of features, and it is this constellation that marks a speaker as from a specific place. So the presence of BAG and BEG tensing may be something that marks residents of Oregon and Washington, but potentially other features also mark either or both locales.

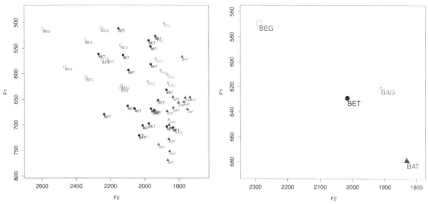

Fig. 8.3. An Oregonian with BAG and BEG tensing. The plot on the left shows the words from four word classes: bag contrasted with bat (words with the same vowel but not before /g/) and beg contrasted with bet (words with the same vowel but not before /g/). The plot on the right shows the mean values for each class. For this speaker, bag and beg are significantly higher and fronter than their respective non-pre-/g/ counterparts.

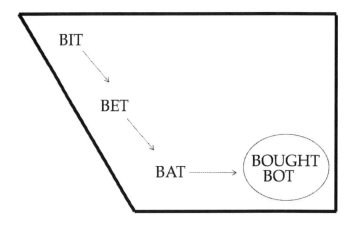

Fig. 8.4. The Short Front Vowel Shift. The merger of the low back vowels bot and bought triggers a chain shift in which bit, bet, and bat rotate down and back in the vowel space.

As noted above, recent research along the West Coast has sought to combat the characterization of the West, from the *Atlas*, as lacking in dialect distinction. To the south of Oregon in California, and to the north of Oregon in Canada, scholars have identified a rotation of a set of vowels, or a vowel shift, that involves the vowels in the vowel classes BIT, BET, and BAT. As depicted by the arrows in figure 8.3, speakers with this Short Front Vowel Shift produce these vowels in a different location in the vowel space than how they are produced by a speaker of mainstream American English. For example, a word like *dad* is pronounced more like "dod," and a word like *hit* is pronounced more like "het." In California, scholars first noted this shift in the 1980s (Hinton et al. 1987), and it has been documented across the state, from the urban west to the rural inland areas to the east, and from Southern California north to San Francisco (Eckert 2008; Kennedy and Grama 2012; Podesva 2011). This shift is phonologically identical to the so-called Canadian Vowel Shift, which has been extensively described by scholars working across Canada (Boberg 2005; Roeder and Jarmasz 2009). In fact, these are likely same shift, which occurs in North American dialects that have merged the low back vowels BOT and BOUGHT. Indeed, there is increasing evidence that this shift exists or is emerging in many areas with low back merger, ranging from Alaska (Bowie et al. 2012) to Illinois (Bigham 2010), and even evidence that it is emerging in Seattle (Swan 2016).

In our research, we found that Oregonians are at an early stage of adoption of the Short Front Vowel Shift (shown in figure 8.4). Their usage is considered to be at an early stage because most speakers don't rotate all of the vowels; rather, many speakers rotate BAT, fewer rotate BET, and fewer still rotate BIT. This would be unsurprising if the shift operates as a

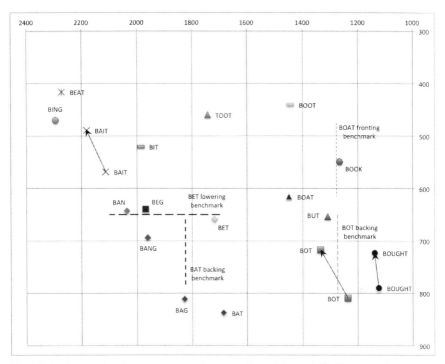

Fig. 8.5. An Oregonian showing an emerging Short Front Vowel Shift. The mean for BAT is far bac ker than the expectation for a non-shifted speaker, while the mean for BET is slightly lower, and the mean for BIT is below bait.

chain, where the low back merger first pulls BAT, then BET, then BIT into the spaces left open in the vowel system (shown in figure 8.5). So the pattern suggests an early stage of the Short Front Vowel Shift, and this is supported by looking at a group of speakers who are often seen as "leaders" of linguistic change—young women. Young women lead for the backing of BAT in this sample of Oregonians, suggesting an ongoing change that will spread throughout the community.

The use of the Short Front Vowel Shift by Oregonians is significant for the proposition that there is a PNW dialect, because Wassink (2015, and this volume) has found no evidence of the shift, though the data from Swan (2016) does find the same pattern of emerging shift. In general, when comparing the research from Wassink and colleagues with our Oregon data, we see that both groups are united in the use of BAG and BEG tensing, but that Washingtonians appear far more conservative in their nonparticipation in more widespread North American sound changes. Oregonians, on the other hand, are active participants in broader North American sound changes, from the Short Front Vowel Shift to the fronting of the vowel class BOAT (also evident in the plot in figure 8.5).

One way to begin answering these questions is to look at data from both production and perception. The details from production can best be interpreted in context, by taking into account what linguistic features *mean* to speakers. In determining whether Oregon English is aligned with Washington English and a unified PNW dialect, or is more oriented outward to general West Coast or North American patterns, we need information about how speakers view these varieties and the boundaries between them. In Oregon, it is difficult to ignore the cultural presence of California, just south of Oregon, and the possibility that Oregonians' language use is influenced by their famous neighbor. So we asked, How do Oregonians see their home state's language with reference to their closest neighbors? Do Oregonians believe in a PNW dialect? Do they see their language use as similar to that in California, or different? Perceptual data can round out the picture we get from production.

EVIDENCE FROM PERCEPTION: A UNIFIED PNW

Evidence from perception suggests that Oregonians do in fact see their state as part of a cohesive PNW region. Recall the map in figure 8.1, which demonstrated the ideology of non-accent, or the belief that "everyone talks the same." Many respondents drew these kinds of maps, in which they were

Fig. 8.6. A map from an Oregonian who sees speech in Oregon and Washington as the same and opposed to speech in California.

resistant to the task because they did not feel they could identify any dialect distinction for the region's picture. But not all respondents rejected the task entirely—many did note divisions on the map, and those divisions are important evidence for the beliefs that Oregonians have about dialect divisions in the PNW.

The respondent in figure 8.6 is representative of a subset of respondents who saw Oregon and Washington as the same, and California as different. This respondent does point out that residents of Yakima, Washington, use an intrusive /r/ in the state's name ("Worshington!"), but circles all of the urban areas along the west coasts of both Oregon and Washington and provides the label "same." That pattern is disrupted just south of the border between Oregon and California, though, when a line is drawn with the label "Different!" Clearly, many Oregonians believe that speech in Oregon in Washington is unified, whereas language use in California is something else entirely.

Our research team had anecdotally observed some Oregonians who spoke negatively of California, resented its cultural presence, and sought to make sure we understood that Oregonians should not be lumped together with the Valley girls and surfers. And indeed, research on California English makes it clear that cultural stereotypes are linked to features of California English, including the Short Front Vowel Shift but also additional features

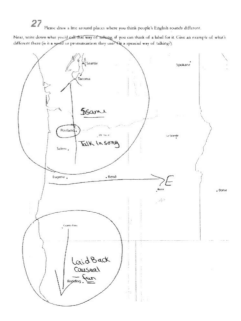

Fig. 8.7. A map from an Oregonian who distinguished Oregon and Washington from California and who views California positively.

like the fronting of the back vowels in words like *boot*, *boat*, and *book*. These vowels are strongly associated with California stereotypes or personae such as the Valley girl and the surfer dude (D'Onofrio 2015), and can be heard regularly in parodies of the state's residents.

As such, we expected to find negative labels used for California speech on the map task. Surprisingly, we observed no such negative labels, and instead saw that when respondents described California, they did so in a positive light. Figure 8.7 is an example of this; this respondent is similar to the respondent in figure 8.6 in opposing a unified Oregon/Washington are to California, but says more than that California is different. For this respondent, California is "laid back, casual, <u>fun</u>."

In addition to looking at the general trend of Oregonians seeing the PNW as unified in perception, we also looked at the relationship between perception and production in Oregon English. Specifically, respondents were placed into two groups: those who expressed the ideology of non-accent on their map (for instance, the speaker in figure 8.1) versus those who did not express this ideology on their map. Interestingly, the respondents with an ideology of non-accent were more likely to produce BAG and BEG tensing, and less likely to produce the rotated vowels of the Short Front Vowel Shift. This is quite significant for the question of a unified PNW dialect. Oregonians who hold the ideology of non-accent in perception—the notion that "everyone talks the same" in the PNW—produce the very feature suggested to mark a PNW dialect, BAG and BEG tensing. In addition, they are less likely to produce the vowel rotation that links Oregon English to the broader patterns found in the West Coast and beyond. Basically, the more you believe in a unified PNW English, the more you use language to identify with that local, unified PNW dialect.

In sum, Oregonians' beliefs and attitudes in perception in some ways contradict their language production. Despite adopting the Short Front Vowel Shift found in California and beyond, they view California language use as overall different than the PNW, though many do see California in a positive light, which might ultimately affect how quickly Oregonians advance toward further adoption of the shift. Oregonians also overall view Oregon and Washington as "the same," in terms of language use, which aligns with the overall picture of BAG and BEG tensing. It is of note, though, that no respondents actually noted this feature on their map task. Could this be because Oregonians are slowly decreasing their use of this feature, such that it is not noticeable? Or, could it be that the feature is one that speakers are simply not very aware of, regardless of how frequent it is in production? Of course, the same observation can be made of the Short Front Vowel Shift—no respondents noted these pronunciations on their map. Instead, Oregonians seem to have a broad sense of language distinction in the PNW, noting which areas are the same or different in speech without providing specific details.

CONCLUSION

Not everyone talks the same in the PNW; our Oregonians' speech production is a unique blend of local and regional features. They use BAG and BEG tensing, linking them to Washingtonians in their use of this distinctly PNW feature. They also produce the Short Front Vowel Shift, adopting this ongoing change that predominates in California, Canada, and elsewhere and may allow Oregonians to access the "fun, laid back" qualities of the California lifestyle. But although they look different from the Washingtonians in Wassink (2015, and this volume) in their production, they nevertheless believe in a unified PNW dialect region, either in expressing an overall ideology of non-accent—that there is no dialect distinction in the PNW—or in noting that Oregon and Washington are the same for language use while California is different. What's more, Oregonian's attitudes and perceptions relate to their language production—respondents with the ideology of non-accent are more likely to produce BAG and BEG tensing and less likely to produce the Short Front Vowel Shift.

In terms of a cohesive PNW dialect, based on the evidence here, the jury is still out. Oregonians align with Washingtonians for BAG and BEG tensing, but are also adopting the Short Front Vowel Shift and use BOAT fronting. Further, it remains to be seen whether BAG and BEG tensing will persist in the PNW or if it is instead in recession. Despite these details as to what Oregonians *say*, though, Oregonians *believe* in a cohesive PNW dialect and, given the potential for language ideologies to affect language change, only time will tell if that perceptual belief will affect language production, further uniting the PNW into a unique dialect region.

References

Becker, Kara, Anna Aden, Katelyn Best, and Haley Jacobson. 2016. "Variation in West Coast English: The Case of Oregon." In *Speech in the Western*

States, edited by V. Fridland, T. Kendall, A. B. Wassink, and B. Evans. American Dialect Society.

Bigham, Douglas S. 2010. "Correlation of the Low-Back Vowel Merger and TRAP-Retraction." *University of Pennsylvania Working Papers in Linguistics* 15 (2).

Boberg, Charles. 2005. "The Canadian Shift in Montreal." *Language Variation and Change* 17 (2): 133–154.

Bowie, David, Tracy Bushnell, Allison Collins, Peter Kudenov, Stacie Meisner, Melissa Ray,. . . Katie Kubitskey. 2012. A Very Northern California Shift? The Vowel System of Southcentral Alaska. Paper presented at the New Ways of Analyzing Variation (NWAV).

D'Onofrio, Annette. 2015. "Perceiving Personae: Effects of Social Information on Perceptions of TRAP-Backing." *University of Pennsylvania Working Papers in Linguistics* 21 (2).

Eckert, Penelope. 2008. "Where Do Ethnolects Stop?" *International Journal of Bilingualism* 12 (1/2): 25–42.

Evans, Betsy. 2013. "'Everybody Sounds the Same': Otherwise Overlooked Ideology in Perceptual Dialectology." *American Speech* 88 (1): 62–80.

Freeman, Valerie. 2013. *Bag, Beg, Bagel: Prevelar Raising and Merger.* Master's thesis, University of Washington, Seattle.

Hartley, Laura C. 1999. "A View from the West: Perceptions of U.S. Dialects by Oregon Residents." In *Handbook of Perceptual Dialectology*, edited by D. R. Preston, 315–332. Amsterdam: John Benjamins.

Hinton, Leanne, Birch Moonwoman, Sue Brennar, Herb Luthin, Mary Van Clay, Jean Lerner, and Hazel Corcoran. 1987. "'It's Not Just the Valley Girls': A Study of California English." *Proceedings of the Thirteenth Annual Meeting of the Berkeley Linguistics Society*, 117–128. https://journals. linguisticsociety.org/proceedings/index.php/BLS/article/view/1834/0.

Kennedy, Robert, and James Grama. 2012. "Chain Shifting and Centralization in California Vowels: An Acoustic Analysis." *American Speech* 87 (1): 39–56.

Labov, William, Sharon Ash, and Charles Boberg. 2006. *The Atlas of North American English: Phonetics, Phonology, and Sound Change.* Berlin: Mouton de Gruyter.

Lippi-Green, Rosina. 1997. *English with an Accent: Language, Ideology, and Discrimination in the United States.* New York: Routledge.

Niedzielski, Nancy A., and Dennis R. Preston. 2003. *Folk Linguistics.* Berlin: Mouton de Gruyter.

Podesva, Robert J. 2011. "The California Vowel Shift and Gay Identity." *American Speech* 86 (1): 32–51.

Preston, Dennis R. 2002. "Language with an Attitude." In *The Handbook of Language Variation and Change*, edited by J. K. Chambers, P. Trudgill, and N. Schilling-Estes, 40–66. Cambridge, UK: Cambridge University Press.

Roeder, Rebecca, and Lidia-Gabriela Jarmasz. 2009. "The Lax Vowel Subsystem in Canadian English Revisited." *Toronto Working Papers in Linguistics* 31:1–12.

Swan, Julia Thomas. 2016. "The Effect of Language Ideologies on the Canadian Shift: Evidence from /ae/ in Vancouver, B.C., and Seattle, WA." *International Journal of Language and Linguistics* 3 (6).

Wassink, Alicia Beckford. 2015. "Sociolinguistic Patterns in Seattle English." *Language Variation and Change* 27:31–58.

PART 4

Perceptions, Pragmatics, and Power

KRISTIN DENHAM

In these final chapters, the authors further explore ways that our perceptions and attitudes about people are intertwined with their language(s) and what those perceptions and attitudes can reveal about the speakers, those who judge them, and the wider societal biases and power differentials that underlie many linguistic views.

In chapter 9, "It's Not What We Say; It's How We Say It: A Pragmatic Overview," Jordan B. Sandoval offers examples of and commentary on socially constructed rules of language use, including the Seattle Nice, Seattle Freeze, and Seattle No, which can distinguish speakers of the Pacific Northwest region. These differences in the language varieties' pragmatics component of grammar can reveal more about how speakers use language to communicate and create identities.

In chapter 10, "Language and Power, Language and Place," Kristin Denham examines broader patterns of language variation and language attitudes to provide more context for the conversations about language in the region. She discusses how assumptions about language and region can reveal discriminatory attitudes that can then lead to unfair practices or even laws about language, though an exploration of official-English laws. She also provides a brief history of settlement patterns of English speakers in order to more fully examine how the varying attitudes toward linguistic variations stem from attitudes toward the speakers, rather than from linguistic facts about the varieties. She brings together many of the threads of the previous chapters, exploring how power dynamics have had effects on people and their languages and cultures as a result of colonization, settlement, and assimilation, and posits that a full understanding of those influences is important as part of exploration of language and culture in the Pacific Northwest.

9
It's Not What We Say; It's How We Say It
A Pragmatic Overview

JORDAN B. SANDOVAL

Previous chapters in this book have discussed a number of unique characteristics of the language and language attitudes of the Pacific Northwest.
To start, speakers of American English in the Pacific Northwest exhibit
linguistic security, often claiming that the way they and others like them
speak is free of any accent and representative of a "standard" American
dialect or variety. In fact, attempts to define "Standard American English"
(SAE) often describe this concept as a variety lacking marked linguistic
features: that is to say, a variety without the stigmatized r-less-ness of New
England, without the Southern drawl, absent the syntactic features of be-
dropping and multiple negation associated with African American English,
lacking the characteristic vowel shift of the Northern Cities region.

In contrast to these varieties, little to no social stigma is associated with
the linguistic variety and speakers of the Pacific Northwest region, which
contributes significantly to the linguistic pride many speakers of this region
exhibit. This attitude blinds many speakers in this region to the unique
linguistic features actually present in their variety, but as we've seen in the
previous chapters, many are quick to note perceived differences between
Washington and Oregon, or across the west/east divide of the Cascade
Range in Washington State. These actual differences are highlighted by
Becker (this volume), who shows that speakers in Oregon are gaining some
vowel characteristics associated with California; by Richardson (this volume), who shows how place-names have their nascence in our Indigenous
and immigrant populations; and by Wassink (this volume), who offers that
there is no one homogeneous monolithic PNW variety, but rather a number of different varieties perceived and produced throughout the region.

This chapter adds two new facets to the previous discussion: exploration of the unique style of Northwest Washington centered around Seattle, and an emphasis not on the phonetic (sounds) or lexical (words) aspects of language differentiation, but on the pragmatic and sociolinguistic aspects—how speakers use language to communicate and create identities. Little academic research has been done in this domain, relative to the emphasis placed on other aspects. A significant amount of popular culture, however, references this unique contribution to Pacific Northwest voices.

New transplants to the region as well as longtime residents are familiar with the terms Seattle Nice, Seattle Freeze, and Seattle No. Despite the city name in these titles, the behavior they reference is commonplace all along the urban I-5 corridor. "Seattle nice" refers to the surface politeness encountered by visitors to the region, exemplified in friendly driving behavior and pleasant encounters with strangers on the street. The "Seattle freeze" is a term given to the difficulty one experiences breaking through the icy veneer of that superficial politeness and forging friendships with native or longtime residents. The "Seattle no" is one linguistic mechanism that transplants to the region recognize as contributing to the difficulty they experience in melting the freeze; we have a common uniquely prevalent indirect method of saying no to invitations and overtures of friendship and other activity prompts.[1]

While each of these behaviors has been addressed individually in blog posts, newspaper articles, and other media, this chapter seeks to provide a unified explanation of these social aspects of one region within the Pacific Northwest as driven by the pragmatics part of the grammar of this regional dialect. It should be noted that pragmatic components of grammar have been often cited as contributing to regional and social variation across American English. There are at least two other regional varieties in the United States that are saliently characterized by pragmatic aspects of their grammars. Consider the stereotypes associated with the speech of New York. Media as well as academic descriptions of the variety point out how New Yorkers establish solidarity within the region through "mutual complaining," through interruption, through rapid-fire questions, and by striking up conversations with strangers (Tannen 1986). Consider also the perception of Southern speakers as exceptionally polite and hospitable— where "bless your heart" can actually be an insult, and where the slow rate of speech is said to reflect a relaxed and deliberative movement through life (Kolker et al. 1987). When New Yorkers are said to be "rude and interrupt a lot," or Southerners are called out as overly solicitous and manifesting hospitality in their language, these are allusions to socially constructed rules of language use that set these communities apart—in other words, differences in the language varieties' pragmatics component of grammar.

POLITENESS AND FACE

In 1978, Brown and Levinson applied the notion of "face" (first introduced by Goffman 1959) to the discourse in the field of pragmatics, particularly how our needs of public perception play a significant role in how politeness is manifest linguistically. The authors claimed (1978, 1987) that many interactions between speakers have the potential to damage the speaker or (sometimes and) the hearer's public face. We call these "face threatening acts" or FTAs for short. Consequently, a speaker's linguistic choices are often designed to mitigate that potential damage and are influenced by a desire to attend to two sides of their public "face" needs: (1) positive face—the speaker and hearer's desire to be well thought of by others, and (2) negative face—the want of the speaker and hearer to be free from the imposition of others. Brown and Levinson argue that, since so many interactions have the possibility of being threatening to either the speaker or hearer's positive or negative face, our language reflects our constant attention to face needs, manifesting as politeness.

To explore what this looks like concretely, let's consider a potentially face threatening act: asking someone to give you a ride to an event. Note that asking someone else to drive you somewhere threatens their negative face (who are you to impose on them!), and it also threatens your positive face (you're needy, people don't like that). You might choose to avoid the face threatening act altogether and figure out your own transportation, or you may go ahead with the face threatening act and ask. At this point, you have the choice to either go "on record" with a direct speech act, or go "off record" with an indirect speech act.

This distinction between direct and indirect speech acts comes from another set of linguistic philosophers, J. L. Austin and John Searle, who demonstrate how and why speakers choose between these two types of language performance. Direct speech acts are literal in form: the speaker uses the linguistic form directly corresponding to the meaning intended to be conveyed. Indirect speech acts, on the other hand, allude to the speaker's intended meaning without using the words or structure literally corresponding to the meaning. This places the burden of comprehension on the hearer to gather the speaker's intended meaning. When a parent says to a child, "Have you cleaned your room?" the child might interpret indirectly (correctly, in the case of my children), "You should clean your room."

Recall in our face threatening act above, the speaker has decided to perform the act and is choosing between going on record or off (direct or indirect). An indirect speech act, asking for a ride to the event, might be, "I sure wish I had a ride to the event tonight." The hearer might interpret that as an indirect request to provide said ride. Upon interpreting that, the hearer might then offer a ride to the speaker—objective achieved. In going off record, the speaker has attempted to manage the hearer's negative face needs by not imposing, but hasn't managed their own positive face needs (the speaker is still seen negatively as a needy person).

If the speaker doesn't want to run the risk of the hearer incorrectly interpreting their indirect speech act (and responding, for instance, "I sure hope you find one!"), the speaker might choose instead an on-record direct speech act. In order to address the face needs of the interactants, rather than simply being issued as a command, "You will take me to the party tonight!"(which is incidentally called going "bald-on-record"), this request will likely come with some sort of linguistic politeness. If the politeness is directed at managing positive face needs, it is called positive politeness ("Would you be so kind as to give me a ride tonight?"). If directed at managing negative face needs, it is a negative politeness strategy ("I hate to bother you, but could you give me a ride tonight?").

Crucially, these face needs are argued to be universal, though the relative importance of speaker and hearer's positive and negative face, as well as the strategies used to "save face," might vary from culture to culture, and from language to language. Though it has recently been argued that grounding a discussion of linguistic politeness in Brown and Levinson's face theory might show a markedly western bias, this framework lends some good insight about some of the unique features of the language of Northwest Washington.

SEATTLE NICE

There is no shortage of blog posts and articles arguing for the exaggerated politeness of Seattle residents. The blog *New To Seattle* claims that newcomers develop a "perception that Seattleites tend to hide disagreements and even anger with others they encounter behind a deceptively false show of friendliness that often gets in the way of conflict resolution." In a 2006

Washington Post article, the then mayor of Seattle Greg Nickels claimed that residents' civility toward one another, as well as their obedience of laws and ordinances, is a reflection of their respect for community.

This politeness plays out in our sports fans' cheering: the famed 12s fans of Seahawk support are known for their loudness, but not the crassness exhibited in so many other NFL arenas. This politeness plays out in our driving: visitors frequently comment on how odd it is when driving that drivers sharing the road pause to let in merging traffic, typically with a wave of invitation (and an expectation of a returned wave of thanks). If you're visiting one of the I-5 corridor cities from Seattle to Canada and you find yourself lost, you can just stand at an intersection looking confused. I am not in the minority as one who immediately approaches the stranger to help them find their way.

The above scenarios are examples of behavioral politeness, but it's not clear how this politeness is manifest linguistically. One example of positive politeness strategies employed in interactions in this region is most evident in customer service environments. Upon placing an order at a sit-down restaurant, your choice will likely be met by your server with an enthusiastic "Awesome." This "awesome" response, or its close relatives, "great" and "perfect," are ubiquitous in customer service environments. This exaggerated positive response serves the purpose of confirming the value and wisdom in the customer's or client's request. Turning again to the restaurant, there is a common interaction that takes place, not just in the Northwest, wherein the server checks in with the diners to ensure the food is to their satisfaction: "How is everything treating you?" says the server. The expected response locally is "Great, thanks," or "Awesome, thanks," or, if you're not the hugest fan, "Good, thanks." Visitors to the region may be surprised to encounter the stigma associated with an overt complaint about the service or food quality.

Although each of these examples, both behavioral and linguistic, are aimed at preserving the positive face needs of interactants, a more thoughtful exploration of the unique characteristics of politeness expressed linguistically in this region within the Pacific Northwest requires that we turn to the other facet of this apparent friendliness, known as the Seattle Freeze.

SEATTLE FREEZE

Just as there is a significant amount of online and print discussion about the characteristics of Seattleite behavior known as Seattle Nice, there is an even greater presence addressing what is referred to as the Seattle Freeze. Many newcomers to this region find that while their new neighbors are perfectly polite and cordial, that veneer of friendliness is impossible to crack, to break into more substantial friendships and authenticity. Invitations to spend time together and to get to know potential new friends are often not followed through with. This difficulty experienced by those new to Seattle who are seeking to break through that perceived iciness has been addressed through the creation of a social organization called the Seattle Anti-Freeze, where social events are advertised and coordinated by people expressing frustration with what is known as the Freeze. This social meet-up group was created in 2006, shortly after a piece was published in the *Seattle Times* on the Freeze, and currently has over ten thousand members.

This disjoint—apparent friendliness coupled with an unwillingness to engage beyond superficial pleasantries—has many transplants to the region mystified. I argue that much of the confusion stems from a communicative misunderstanding in socio-pragmatic aspects of cross-dialectical dialogue: in nontechnical jargon, people who don't speak this variety of Pacific Northwest English don't understand the communicative function of some politeness strategies employed by speakers here. To concretely illustrate this communicative difficulty, we turn to another familiar Seattle expression, the Seattle No.

SEATTLE NO

The Seattle No refers to the indirect speech act folks here use to avoid directly declining a proposition. If you ask a person if they want to go see a show with you, and they respond, "That sounds interesting, I'll have to check my calendar," in Seattle this means no. If the response is, "Maybe," that too means no. If they say, "Send me an e-mail about it!" that means no. If you ask via a text or e-mail or leave the invitation in voicemail and you don't hear back, that means no as well.

It is clear that the motivation for this type of indirect speech act is also driven by a consideration of public perception of the interactants' face. A google search on "how to say no without saying no" reveals some of the underlying reasons a person might choose an indirect speech act for this communicative intent. "How to say no to your boss," "Saying no in Customer Service," "7 ways to say no without making people mad"—each of these headlines highlights the social relationships between the one saying no and the one to whom they are saying so. In each instance, indirect ways of communicating "no" are said to those in a (potentially) more powerful position. Female students in my linguistics classes (Western Washington University) have cited indirect "no"s as commonplace in their interactions with would-be suitors, as they navigate the expected (and sometimes dangerous) reactions to direct declinations.[2]

At the heart of each of these indirect communications of "no" is a recognition of the importance of the other's positive face. Saying no to someone threatens their positive face (their desire to be well thought of). In order to save their public face, the speaker allows the listener to interpret a no, while never actually saying no. This allows the two in conversation to, as linguist Steven Pinker (2007) puts it, "preserve the fiction of friendship".

You may ask how someone can say "yes" if they actually do need to check their calendar, or need an e-mail follow-up about the event. Typically, this is encoded as follows: "That sounds interesting, I'll have to check my calendar. I really actually do want to go with you, and I'll get back to you if it works within the next day." Or, even more directly, pulling out the calendar just then and there and setting the date.

LACK OF AWARENESS

Longtime residents typically aren't aware of the specific ways their pragmatic component of grammar is differently organized from other regions until a speaker from another dialect or visitor from another culture highlights the differences. It is typically true of non-stigmatized linguistic varieties that speakers don't realize in what ways their dialect varies from what they would call a "standard" variety of the language until their use is called out as unique among others. This ties in to the discussion of self-awareness and prestige associated with the varieties spoken, especially west of the Cascades, in Washington State.

EXPLANATION

This social behavior and the language through which it is manifest has been argued to stem from a number of different, potentially overlapping, sources. Some argue that the high numbers of Scandinavian immigrants, known for their self-reliance, have influenced the behavior of the communities at large. Others highlight the role of Japanese immigrant populations and their polite, reserved nature. Inasmuch as the outcome of the Freeze and the No results in difficulty creating and maintaining a large set of friendships, the technical industry centered on Microsoft's home and the many thousands of introverted tech nerd employees in residence (who are, according to this explanation, happy to not gain any new friends) are also blamed. Yet another explanation for the polite linguistic behavior, apparently unconcerned with nailing down specific activity plans, is attributed to the prevalence of (recently legalized) marijuana use and the habits of the stereotypical stoned laid-back hippie. Lastly, the weather has attracted its share of blame—the dreary rainy and cold weather for nine months of the year confines residents to their houses, fireplaces, and books.

In this chapter I argue that some combination of the above has led to a particular ranking and cultural understanding of positive and negative face needs of residents. And further, that speakers of this variety are (often unconsciously) adhering to these rules, thereby creating a culturally unique identity—that of the Pacific Northwest, centered around the urban I-5 corridor. The cultural agreements, however unconscious, result in the discussed linguistic manifestations of politeness, explainable through reference to what linguists call pragmatics.

So, although speakers in the Pacific Northwest, as well as those commenting on the region, don't often criticize or even recognize the linguistic features that set this region apart, there are nonetheless unique characteristics of the language that can be addressed. We make assumptions about specific cultures, and sometimes the individuals that make up that culture, on the basis of our preconceived associations with aspects of their language. When we call New Yorkers rude, or Southerners slow, or Seattleites frigid, we should question whether those assumptions are fair. Observing the speech patterns of different regions allows us to utilize the tools of linguistic analysis, making more transparent the connections among language, culture, and identity. Cross-cultural misunderstanding and unfair judgment are more likely to arise when we lack an understanding of the linguistic and cultural conventions that set each speech community apart. A study of language and culture, analyzed through the linguistic domain of pragmatics, can help us situate the Pacific Northwest within this country's great linguistic diversity.

Notes

1 I use "we" here and throughout, as I am a member of this speech community and a speaker of this variety of Pacific Northwest American English.

2 This particular motivation and context for indirect expressions of "no" is not limited to Seattle or the PNW region at all. A quote from an article titled "Why Women Have a Hard Time Saying No" on the popular *Psychology Today* blog illustrates the pressure many females in particular feel to succumb to societal norms of gender and power: "So, whatever you do, don't do or say anything that will trigger the male ego. We know that may seem like an impossible charge, but do your best."

References

American Tongues: A Film about the Way We Talk. Film. Directed by Louis Alvarez and Andy Kolker. 56 min. New York: Center for New American Media. http://luckysoap.com/thegatheringcloud/

Austin, J. L. 1962. *How to Do Things with Words*. London: Oxford University Press.

Barrett, W. P. 2014. "Fresh Proof of 'Seattle Freeze' and 'Seattle Nice.'" *New To Seattle*, February 26. www.newtoseattle.com.

Brown, P., and S. Levinson. 1978. "Universals in Language Usage: Politeness Phenomena." In *Questions and Politeness*, edited by E. Goody, 56–310. Cambridge, UK: Cambridge University Press.

Brown, P., and S. Levinson. 1987. *Politeness: Some Universals in Language Use*. Cambridge, UK: Cambridge University Press.

Goffman, E. 1959. *The Presentation of Self in Everyday Life*. New York: Anchor.

Hardin, B. 2006. "In Seattle, the Hostile Crowd Is All Smiles." January 13, *Washington Post*.

Pinker, S. 2007. *The Stuff of Thought: Language as a Window into Human Nature*. New York: Viking.

Searle, J. 1969. *Speech Acts*. Cambridge, UK: Cambridge University Press.

Searle, J. 1975. "Indirect Speech Acts." In *Syntax and Semantics*, vol. 3, *Speech Acts*, edited by P. Cole and J. L. Morgan, 59–82. New York: Academic Press.

Tannen, D. 1986. "Talking New York: It's Not What You Say; It's The Way That You Say It." In *Language Power*, edited by D. Seyler. New York: Random House.

Vilkki, L. 2006. "Politeness, Face and Facework: Current Issues." In *Festschrift in Honour of Fred Karlsson*, edited by M. Suominen, A. Arppe, A. Airola, O. Heinämäki, M. Miestamo, U. Määttä, J. Niemi, K. K. Pitkänen, and K. Sinnemäki, 322–332. Turku: Linguistics Association of Finland.

10
Language and Power, Language and Place
KRISTIN DENHAM

Language and place are intimately linked, and this volume highlights that. We have explored the many varied voices of those who live or have lived in what some call the Pacific Northwest region. But it's also important to explore the ways in which making assumptions about language and region can reveal discriminatory attitudes or can lead to unfair assumptions or even laws about language. Language and identity are closely linked, so an attack on someone's language or their language variety is an attack on a person. Such attacks on language can be subtle and even unintentional, but they always have repercussions.

EFFECTS OF LANGUAGE LAWS AND POLICIES
The idea that a nation has a single language is a unique idea among the world's nations; most people in the world are not just bilingual, but multilingual. Estimates vary, but it's generally agreed that more than half of the world's population uses more than one language on a daily basis (Grosjean 2010). The United States, however, remains what we consider to be a monolingual nation, with some 97 percent of the population speaking English well. Such is the power of colonization, and the chapters in part 2 of this volume explored the reasons for this and the ways in which Indigenous voices are rising up.

Also, the percentage of people who are bilingual is on the rise: it is currently about 20 percent, a figure that has doubled since 1980 (US Census Bureau n.d.). Although multilingualism is often viewed as an asset outside of the United States, it is sometimes met with suspicion within the country. The education system in the United States seems to recognize that some language study is important, but the teaching of languages other than English, and the recognition of its importance, is not prioritized by most school districts. Typically instruction in a second language doesn't happen until high school, by which point it becomes much more difficult to learn. In general, there is little funding for or commitment to second-language teaching or for bilingual or immersion programs. At most, only 3 percent of elementary children are enrolled in bilingual programs today (Goldenberg and Wagner 2015), and this percentage is half of what it was in 1900 (Kloss 1977). The many reasons for this situation are beyond the scope of this chapter, but opposition to bi- and multilingualism has long correlated with anti-immigrant stances. Nativist opposition to the use of languages other than English peaked after World War I, targeting especially German, but also other languages (for a wealth of information on this topic, see, for starters, Baker 2011 and Crawford 1995). We see anti-immigration attitudes correlating with opposition to languages other than English again today in the various legislative attempts to make English an official language, often to the exclusion of other languages.

Despite the ubiquity of English in the United States, there is periodically but consistently a push for legislation to make English the official language of the country. And although the United States does not have and has never had an official language, many states do have laws making English the official language (the current count is thirty-two).[1] Neither Oregon nor Washington has an official-English law. Note that most of these laws have been made since the 1980s; the number of states with laws making English the official language has doubled since the 1990s. US English, a "non-partisan citizens' action group dedicated to preserving the unifying role of the English language in the United States" (US English), promotes the idea that an official language can serve to unify. However, unity stemming from laws regulating languages is not borne out by evidence in the history of either the United States or other countries; in fact, the laws can instead be divisive. The American Civil Liberties Union offers a brief history of attitudes toward languages other than English in the United States:

> At the time of the nation's founding, it was commonplace to hear as many as 20 languages spoken in daily life, including Dutch, French, German and numerous Native American languages. Even the Articles of Confederation were printed in German, as well as English. During the 19th and early 20th centuries, the nation's linguistic diversity grew as successive waves of Europeans immigrated to these shores and U.S. territory expanded to include

Puerto Rico, Hawaii and the Philippines. (Briefing Paper no. 6, "English Only")

The effects of the official-English laws in each state are quite varied, but some of them include elimination of services in languages other than English in areas such as health, education, social welfare services, job training, translation assistance for crime victims and witnesses in court, court administrative proceedings, voting registration, voting ballots, and driver's license exams. Some state laws apply not only to government, but also to private businesses. Several Southern California cities passed ordinances that restrict the use of languages other than English on private business signs. Some have opposed licensing of Spanish-language radio stations and even bilingual menus at restaurants. It cannot be denied that many campaigns for restricting other languages target primarily Latinos and Asians, who make up the majority of recent immigrants.

Despite immigration by speakers of languages other than English into the United States, the vast majority of US residents speak English well, which is, according to Nunberg (1997), "a level of linguistic homogeneity unsurpassed by any other large nation in history" (41). English is certainly not threatened, and immigrants are learning English faster than any other group of non-English-speaking immigrants in history: Nunberg, citing the demographer Calvin Veltman, states that the traditional three-generation period for a complete shift to English is being shortened to two generations. Nunberg also references another study showing that more than 90% of first-generation Hispanics born in California have native fluency in English and only 50% of the second generation still speak Spanish (Nunberg 1997).

The numbers of speakers of languages other than English does continue to rise in the United States and in the Pacific Northwest as well. Consider Spanish in Washington and Oregon: the map in figure 10.1 shows the number of people who report speaking Spanish as their primary language in the 2011 American Community Survey in Washington and Oregon, based on US Census Bureau (n.d.) figures.

The higher density of dots in the map, representing speakers of Spanish, clusters in the agriculture regions of southeastern Washington and of north-central Oregon's Hood River Valley (where there are also speakers of other languages such as Mixteco and Mam; see, for example, Geyman et al. 2011). Any discussion of Northwest voices should recognize these voices and consider the important ways in which language and identity

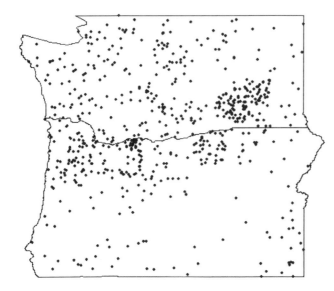

Fig. 10.1. Spanish language, 2006–2010, by county. (Data from the American Community Survey 2006–2010, five-year estimates, table DP02, "Selected Social Characteristics in the United States," one dot = 1000 people. Thanks to Logan Matz, Leah Sharaby, and Rob Rich for help with the mapping.)

are intertwined and how suppression of one language in favor of another always has consequences. We should also consider how bilingualism and multilingualism are assets, rather than liabilities, and need not be feared and regulated. Bilingualism is beneficial not only for fostering a sense of identity and community, but also for providing other benefits: for example, there is much evidence for enhanced cognitive functions stemming from bilingualism (see, for example, Bialystok et al. 2004, 2014; Bialystok, Craik, and Luk 2008; Costa, Hernández, and Sebastián-Gallés 2008; Adesope et al. 2010). Thus, our schools, our legislators, and our communities could examine ways in which advocating for other languages in various ways can, in fact, serve to unify.

This brief overview of English-language policies and legislation illus-trates the ubiquity of English in the United States and reveals the impor-tant ways in which policies, laws, and attitudes surrounding language affect us and affect our language use. And while there appears to be no cause for concern that speakers of languages other than English can threaten English—its dominance remains undisputed—there may be ways in which the shifting demographics could affect our governmental and educational policies. Past policies drove the languages of the Indigenous peoples into hiding or into oblivion, as discussed in previous chapters. And current policies about language may affect people's civil rights, the languages they use at home, and certainly the languages used in school. Even when the language in question is English, our attitudes and policies about *which* English come into play.

AMERICAN DIALECTS PAST AND PRESENT AND THE MYTH OF "STANDARD ENGLISH"

Battistella and Pippin (this volume) discuss the history of the peoples of the Pacific Northwest. Here, I briefly explore the settlement history of the larger United States to better understand how English variants arise. The first permanent English settlements in the area that was to become the United States were on the east coast of North America, in Jamestown, Virginia, beginning in 1607, and in Plymouth, Massachusetts, beginning in 1620. Although we know that these settlers, most of whom were seeking religious freedom, were from England, we don't know precisely where most of them came from within England. They likely spoke a wide variety of dialects, and features of those can still be detected in varieties of English along the East Coast. Throughout the seventeenth and eighteenth centuries, many more immigrants came to North America, settling along the Eastern Seaboard; the speech of these new Americans, with many distinct languages and dialects, began to blend, and this melding process of American English continued throughout the nineteenth and twentieth centuries as people migrated westward. A dialect map like the one shown in figure 10.2 illustrates how the dialect distinctions diminished as

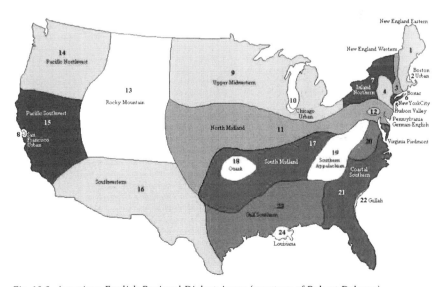

Fig. 10.2. American English Regional Dialect Areas (courtesy of Robert Delaney)

migration of English speakers spread westward. The largest group of the European settlers to the Pacific Northwest came from Illinois, Missouri, Indiana, Ohio, and Massachusetts (Reed 1952).

But in fact, although the distinctions among regional dialects may have diminished to some extent, a wide range of distinctions still remains among the many varieties of English spoken in the United States (and elsewhere around the globe), including the Pacific Northwest, as we have explored throughout the volume. When Americans became more mobile and gained widespread access to broadcasting in the mid-twentieth century, many thought that dialect distinctions would disappear and a single standardized version of English would emerge. This has not happened, however. The importance of preferring to sound like those around you, like those you identify with, like those in your "in-group," is a much more powerful motivator for language conformity than the desire to sound like a newscaster or a pedantic teacher. So dialectal variations among the language we call English are alive and well. We've seen throughout this book ways in which the English of the Pacific Northwest is distinguishing itself from other varieties. Research such as Wassink's (this volume) shows that there are features of the English of the region that distinguish it from the English of other parts of the country. As the contributions from Evans (this volume) and Becker (this volume) note, however, many speakers of English in the Pacific Northwest region don't think they have a dialect; many claim they speak without an "accent." As Becker notes, most speakers of English who hail from the Pacific Northwest enjoy a high level of linguistic security.

In order to understand the perceived lack of dialect, we must consider what we mean when we say that someone has an accent or a dialect. What are we comparing it to? Our own dialect? Some standardized variety? Whose? The fact is, there is no true or single standard variety of English. We have really no more than a couple of handfuls of words, pronunciations, and grammatical constructions that we might associate with "nonstandard" English, and these are actually few and far between. And these handfuls of shibboleths really belie much more about our attitudes toward marginalized groups than about language (see, for example, Baugh 2000; Lippi-Green 2012; Alim, Rickford, and Ball 2016). The vowel shifts described in chapters by Wassink and Becker that affect words like *bag* and *beg* are typically not stigmatized or even noticed by speakers from elsewhere, whereas the way in which a speaker from, say, Alabama might pronounce a word like *fire* more like "far," or an African American might pronounce *ask* more like "aks," are noticed by speakers outside of those speech communities and are typically labeled "nonstandard." But who decides what's standard? It's not determined by what's more successful communicatively—all of these variations do that really well—but instead by who wields the power. As Sandoval (this volume) notes, stigmatized varieties are spoken by those with less power, those who are marginalized. English speakers in the Pacific Northwest, historically, have not been marginalized and have been largely white; therefore, their speech is not marginalized. We have seen some examples of stigmatized language even within the "linguistically secure" Pacific Northwest. Evans (this volume) notes the pronunciation of *Washington* as if it has an /r/, sounding more like "Warshington."[2] This pronunciation is not just found in Washington, but in (mostly rural) communities all over the country and other parts of the English-speaking world. The insertion of /r/ in pronunciation is viewed as quaint if British: "the very idear of it," "sawr it over there," but as a stigmatized class marker if found in the rural United States.

So it's important to examine our attitudes about variation before jumping to judgment, and to consider what we are comparing to when saying that someone does or does not have an accent or a particular dialect—and to really reflect on why the English spoken by many in the Pacific Northwest is not stigmatized: its speakers are not stigmatized.

ON BORDERS AND BOUNDARIES

Viewing the people of a region via a language lens can reveal ways in which language, identity, and place are all intertwined. Our region has official borders and also unofficial boundaries of other sorts—real and imagined, geopolitical and geographical—and languages and dialects sometimes pay those a bit of mind. Borders can result in varied notions of identity and can therefore lead to differences in language. Actual physical boundaries sometimes separate one language variety from another. In New England, the Connecticut River long distinguished those who said "park the car" from those who pronounced the same phrase on the other side of the river more like "pahk the cah." Some vocabulary differences respect the British Columbia–Washington State border. The *bathroom* suddenly becomes *the washroom*. The *grocery cart* is the *buggy*. The first syllable of the word *process* rhymes with either *go* or *bra*, depending on which side of the border you live on. These distinctions, of course, are not due to anything that happens at the border itself, but to the ways in which speakers self-identify as Canadian or American, and our subconscious desires to speak like those around us, those members of our communities.

Before there was a Canadian and US border or provincial and state borders, there was still a region—a region with borders defined largely by the natural geographical boundaries of mountains, rivers, and coastline, and the trade routes that followed them. The use of Ichishkiin (also known as Sahaptin) spanned the Columbia River, and Athabaskan languages were spoken across what is now the coastal California and Oregon border, oblivious to these modern-day state boundaries. Spread throughout this region are the speakers of many Indigenous languages. The contributions by Hugo, by Zenk and Cole, and by Miller (all this volume) acknowledge many of these languages, and the place-names throughout the region (Richardson, this volume) are a daily reminder of the peoples who have long lived there. Parts of British Columbia, Washington, Oregon, Idaho, and Montana have been designated as "language hotspots" by National Geographic's Enduring Voices Project and The Living Tongues Institute, an Oregon-based organization devoted to the documentation, mainte-nance, preservation, and revitalization of endangered languages around the world. The region is one of the five hotspots in the world because of its high number of diverse Native languages that are from different "geneti-cally diverse" language groups (as different as English and Italian, in some cases; in others, as different as English and Chinese) that are highly endan-gered. When an entire group of languages is no longer spoken, we lose not only linguistic information that is of great importance to linguists, but also, as Crawford puts it, "The loss of linguistic diversity means a loss of intellectual diversity" (1995, 33). Consider, as an example, ways in which a language can encapsulate certain kinds of knowledge: the Halkomel'em Musqueam people group certain kinds of fish under the "salmon" label: sce:ɫtən. This includes fish that are called steelhead trout and cutthroat trout in English, but which genetic analysis has shown are, in fact, of the salmon genus, and not trout at all. Such information about flora and fauna from peoples who have lived in the region for millennia can disappear right along with the language, as well as, of course, the loss of culture and of identity, which are so closely tied to language. Our languages are impor-tant; each one and its many forms should be carefully considered as an integral part of language and place.

FINAL THOUGHTS

When we examine language, we must examine history as well. We must also understand the shifting power dynamics that have had effects on people and their languages and cultures as a result of colonization, settlement, and assimilation. We must understand that attitudes toward variation within a language have to do with power as well; the stigmatized features of any language variety are not stigmatized because there is anything wrong with them linguistically, but simply because someone with some authority, some power, has told others that the particular feature is "bad," "sloppy," "weird," or "uneducated." An exploration of the languages and language varieties of the Pacific Northwest region must include investigation into the linguistic diversity within a language and among languages. We must strive to understand the role we all play in determining the past, the present, and the future of our linguistic and cultural communities.

Notes

1   Here is the current list, with the dates the laws were established: Alabama, 1990; Alaska, 1998; Arizona, 2006; Arkansas, 1987; California, 1986; Colorado, 1988; Florida, 1988; Georgia, 1986 and 1996; Hawai'i, 1978 (though Hawai'i is the only state with a second official language, Hawaiian); Idaho, 2007; Illinois, 1969; Indiana, 1984; Iowa, 2002; Kansas, 2007; Kentucky, 1984; Louisiana, 1811; Massachusetts, 1975; Mississippi, 1987; Missouri, 1998 and 2008; Montana, 1995; Nebraska, 1920; New Hampshire, 1995; North Carolina, 1987; North Dakota, 1987; Oklahoma, 2010; South Carolina, 1987; South Dakota, 1995; Tennessee, 1984; Utah, 2000; Virginia, 1981 and 1996; Wyoming, 1996; West Virginia, 2016.

2   Many are quick to suggest that one should not pronounce this word with an /r/ because there is not one in the spelling, but beware of resorting to spelling as justification for any particular pronunciation. Do you pronounce the first /l/ in *colonel* as /r/? Do you pronounce the /k/ in *know*? Do you insert a vowel in between the two syllables of *realtor*?

References

Adesope, O. O., T. Lavin, T. Thompson, and C. Ungerleider. 2010. "A Systematic Review and Meta-Analysis of the Cognitive Correlates of Bilingualism." *Review of Educational Research* 80 (245–207 :(2.

Alim, Samy, John Rickford, and Aretha Ball. 2016. *Raciolinguistics: How Language Shapes Our Ideas about Race.* New York: Oxford University Press.

American Civil Liberties Union. 1996. "English Only." Briefing paper. http://www.lectlaw.com/files/con09.htm.

Baker, Colin. 2011. *Foundation of Bilingual Education and Bilingualism.* Bristol, UK: Multilingual Matters.

Baugh, John. 2000. *Beyond Ebonics: Linguistic Pride and Racial Prejudice.* New York: Oxford University Press.

Bialystok, Ellen, Fergus Craik, and Gigi Luk. 2008. "Cognitive Control and Lexical Access in Younger and Older Bilinguals." *Journal of Experimental Psychology: Learning, Memory, and Cognition* 34 *(873–859 :(4.*

Bialystok, Ellen, Fergus I. M. Craik, Raymond Klein, and Mythili Viswanathan. 2004. "Bilingualism, Aging, and Cognitive Control: Evidence from the Simon Task." *Psychology and Aging* 19 *(303–290 :(2.*

Bialystok, Ellen, Gregory Poarch, Lin Luo, and Fergus I. M. Craik. 2014. *"Effects of* Bilingualism and Aging on Executive Function and Working Memory." *Psychology and Aging* 29 (3): 696–705.

Costa, Albert, Mireia Hernández, and Núria Sebastián-Gallés. 2008. "Bilingualism Aids Conflict Resolution: Evidence from the ANT Task." *Cognition* 106 *(86–59 :(1.*

Crawford, James. 1995. *Bilingual Education: History, Politics, Theory, and Practice.* Trenton, NJ: Crane.

Geyman, Matthew, Andrea L. Schmitt, Sarah Leyrer, Daniel G. Ford, Rebecca Smith, and Matt Adams. 2011. "Indigenous Guatemalan and Mexican Workers in Washington State: Living Conditions and Legal Issues." *Mexican Law Review* 5 (1): 41–80.

Goldenberg, Claude, and Kirstin Wagner. 2015. "Bilingual Education: Reviving and American Tradition." *American Educator* 39 (3): 28–32.

Grosjean, François. 2010. *Bilingual: Life and Reality.* Cambridge, MA: Harvard University Press.

Harrison, K. David. 2007. *When Languages Die: The Extinction of the World's Languages and the Erosion of Human Knowledge.* New York: Oxford University Press.

Kloss, Heinz. 1977. *The American Bilingual Tradition.* Rowley, MA: Newbury House.

Lippi-Green, Rosina. 2012. *English with an Accent: Language, Ideology and Discrimination in the United States.* 2nd ed. London: Routledge.

Nunberg, Geoffrey. 1997. "Lingo Jingo." *American Prospect* 8 (33): 40–47.

Reed, Carroll. 1952. "The Pronunciation of English in the State of Washington." *American Speech* 27 (3):186–189.

US Census Bureau, n.d. "Detailed Languages Spoken at Home and Ability to Speak English for the Population 5 Years and Over for United States: 2009–2013." American Community Survey. http://www.census.gov/data/tables/2013/demo/2009-2013-lang-tables.html.

US English. n.d. "Making English the Official Language." https://www.usenglish.org/.

About the Contributors

EDWIN BATTISTELLA is a professor of English at Southern Oregon University in Ashland. He has a PhD in linguistics from the City University of New York. Battistella has also been a visiting researcher at the IBM Research Center in Yorktown Heights, New York, and a visiting faculty member at the Vilem Mathesius Workshop on Linguistics at Charles University in the Czech Republic. His publications include *Sorry About That: The Language of Public Apology*; *Do You Make These Mistakes in English?: The Story of Sherwin Cody's Famous Language School*; *Bad Language: Are Some Words Better Than Others?*; and *The Logic of Markedness* (all from Oxford University Press) and *Markedness: The Evaluative Superstructure of Language* (State University of New York Press). Battistella is a member of the editorial board of the *Oregon Encyclopedia* and has served on the board of directors of Oregon Humanities.

KARA BECKER is associate professor of linguistics at Reed College. She received a BA in linguistics and an MA in educational linguistics from Stanford University, and PhD in linguistics from New York University. She joined the Reed faculty in 2010 and teaches courses on language and society, including Dialects of English; Contact Languages; Language, Sex, Gender and Sexuality; and African American English. Her interests include sociolinguistics, variation and change, dialectology, race/ethnicity, sex/gender/sexuality, and social meaning. Her research focuses on regional and social varieties of American English, most notably New York City English and Oregon English.

KATHY COLE is a *chinuk-wawa* high school and adult language teacher for the Confederated Tribes of Grand Ronde and is also a member of the tribe. Kathy has her teaching license in education and an American Indian Language Teacher license. She has been trained in ACTFL and assesses adult language fluency. She is a member of the American Indian Language Committee for Lane Community College. Kathy has been teaching *chinuk-wawa* for fifteen years. She teaches a high school class at Willamina High, in Oregon, where her students receive college credit through Lane Community College. She co-teaches *chinuk-wawa* classes with instructors from Lane Community College, and she also teaches adult *chinuk-wawa* classes for adults in the community.

KRISTIN DENHAM is professor of linguistics at Western Washington University. She received her BA in lingusitics and French from Swarthmore College, her MA in linguistics from the Univeristy of Arizona, and her PhD in linguistics from the University of Washington (with a dissertation on question formation in an Athabaskan language, Babine-Witsuwit'en). Her primary research agenda involves the integration of linguistic knowledge into K–12 teaching. She is coauthor (with Anne Lobeck) of *Linguistics for Everyone* (Wadsworth, 2013), *Navigating English Grammar* (Wiley-Blackwell, 2014), and *Why Study Linguistics* (Routledge, 2018) and co-editor (also with Anne Lobeck) of *Language in the Schools: Integrating Linguistic Knowledge into K–12 Teaching* (LEA, 2005) and *Linguistics at School: Language Awareness in Primary and Secondary Education* (Cambridge, 2010). A syntactician, she teaches courses on syntax, Salishan languages, language and identity, endangered languages, English grammar, and linguistics in education, and is actively involved in the Linguistic Society of America's Language in the School Curriculum Committee.

BETSY E. EVANS is an associate professor of linguistics at in the Department of Linguistics at the University of Washington. She has a PhD in linguistics from Michigan State University. Her research interests focus on the attitudes and perceptions of language variation and the perceptions of spatial distribution of variation in language. Recent research projects include the collection and analysis of perceptual dialect maps in Washington State (Evans 2011, 2013) and Cardiff, Wales, UK (under review). She is coauthor (with Annabelle Mooney) of *Language, Society and Power*, 4th edition (2015) and 5th edition (in press), and co-editor (with Erica Benson and James Stanford) of *Language Regard: Methods, Variation and Change* (2018).

RUSSELL HUGO is the assistant director of the University of Washington Language Learning Center. He earned his PhD in linguistics from the University of Washington in 2016, with a focus on Indigenous language preservation and revitalization. He is interested in critically examining the integration of technology into such efforts, particularly with concerns regarding the absence or existence of verifiable pedagogical potential, costs, and security concerns. His general academic interests include computer assisted language learning (CALL), language attitudes, formulaic language, and archiving. The University of Washington Language Learning Center is eager to support local community-led Indigenous language revitalization efforts with respect to technology.

DANICA STERUD MILLER grew up on the Puyallup Indian reservation in a highly political Puyallup family, which is reflected in her academic work. Miller received her BA in English and linguistics from Western Washington University, and her PhD in English from Fordham University. An assistant professor of American Indian studies at the University of Washington Tacoma, her work focuses on resistance to federal Indian law in American Indian literature. She is especially interested in how these moments of resistance trace traditional acts of sovereignty. At present, she is writing a book on Puyallup history.

DAVID PIPPIN is a boatbuilding and humanities teacher in the Boston Public Schools system. Prior to teaching in Boston, David lived for two decades in Seattle and on an island in the Salish Sea teaching linguistic inquiry in his middle-school classrooms. He is coauthor (with Maya Honda and Wayne O'Neil) of "On Promoting Linguistics Literacy: Bringing Language Science to the English Classroom" in *Linguistics at School: Language Awareness in Primary and Secondary Education*, edited by Kristin Denham and Anne Lobeck (Cambridge University Press, 2010), and (with Kristin Denham) "Sustained Linguistic Inquiry as a Means of Confronting Language Ideology and Prejudice" in *Teaching Language Variation in the Classroom: Strategies and Models from Teachers and Linguists*, edited by Michelle D. Devereaux and Chris C. Palmer (Routledge, forthcoming). David has presented papers at the annual meeting of the Linguistics Society of America and is a former chair of the LSA's Linguistics in the School Curriculum committee.

ALLAN RICHARDSON received an MA in anthropology from the University of Washington, Seattle, and taught anthropology at Whatcom Community College for thirty-eight years. At Whatcom he also served as department chair of Social and Behavioral Sciences and as coordinator of the Honors Program. He has published articles on Northwest Coast Native culture and has served as consultant to the Nooksack Indian Tribe for a number of grants and legal cases. His work has included completion of a National Register of Historic Places nomination and research in the records of the Northwest Boundary Survey of 1857–1861. Mr. Richardson is coauthor, with Dr. Brent Galloway, of the book *Nooksack Place Names: Geography, Culture, and Language* (University of British Columbia Press, 2011). He is also active in the Washington Native Plant Society and lives on a small farm on the outskirts of Bellingham, Washington.

JORDAN B. SANDOVAL is a senior instructor in linguistics at Western Washington University in Bellingham, Washington. She received her BA in linguistics from Western Washington University and, after completing her PhD from University of Arizona in 2008, returned to teaching at WWU. Her research interests include orthographic influence on lexical representations, language and identity, sex/gender/sexuality, and second language phonological acquisition pedagogy. She teaches courses across a wide variety of topics in language from phonetics to pragmatics, including sociolinguistics, language variation and change, and language and identity. Her book *Thinking Like a Linguist* is forthcoming from Cambridge University Press.

ALICIA BECKFORD WASSINK is associate professor in the Department of Linguistics, University of Washington, and director of the Sociolinguistics Laboratory. She has served as principal investigator of the English in the Pacific Northwest study since 2006. Wassink's research interests lie in production and perception of the time-varying features of vowel systems, language ideology, social network modeling, dialect contact, development of sociolinguistic competence in children, and creole linguistics. Wassink is a past visiting research fellow, University of the West Indies, Mona, Kingston, Jamaica. Her work has appeared in *Speech in the Western States* (Duke University Press), *Language and Identity* (Edinburgh University Press), *African-American Women's Language* (Oxford), *Best Practices in Sociophonetics* (Routledge), and *Language in the Schools* (Elsevier). Primary reports of her research have appeared in *Journal of the Acoustical Society of America, Journal of Phonetics, Language in Society, Language Variation and Change, Journal of English Linguistics*, and the *International Journal of Speech-Language Pathology*.

HENRY ZENK, Oregonian by birth, was introduced to the study of Northwest languages and lifeways by Wayne Suttles, late professor of anthropology at Portland State University. He subsequently documented Chinuk Wawa from elder speakers of the Grand Ronde Indian Community, Oregon, drawing upon his results for his PhD in anthropology from the University of Oregon. Since 1998 he has been working as a linguistic consultant for the Confederated Tribes of Grand Ronde. Besides contributing to a variety of scholarly series and symposia over the years, he compiled and edited *Chinuk Wawa kakwa nsayka ulman-tilixam ɬaska munk-kəmtəks nsayka / Chinuk Wawa as Our Elders Teach Us to Speak It*, a new Chinuk Wawa dictionary published (2012) by the Confederated Tribes of Grand Ronde.

Index

Page numbers with an "n" refer to notes, an "f" to figures, and a "t" to tables.